# Gift Wrapping

Annette Claxton

The Art of Crafts

First published in 2000 by
The Crowood Press Ltd
Ramsbury, Marlborough
Wiltshire SN8 2HR

**British Library Cataloguing-in-Publication Data**
A catalogue record for this book is available from the British Library.

ISBN 1 86126 363 5

**Dedication**
To Robert, for without his unfailing patience, skills and practical help with the makes and photography, I would never have met the deadline; thank you!

My thanks for their generosity in sharing techniques and materials for this book: Fenella Woods (Dylon), Diane Huck (P & Q Stencils), Michelle Huberman (Fashion 'n' Foil Magic), Ali and Tony (Crafty Ribbons), Lucy at C & T Publishing; and to Elaine Thomson, the lovely hand model.

I am also grateful to Anna and Richard from The Pier, Bromley, for the loan of props.

Finally Steve Tanner and his assistant Lucille have once more waved a magic wand and conjured up stunning images. Merci.

Project photography by Robert Claxton
All other photography by Steve Tanner
Templates by Robert Claxton
Illustrations by Annette Findlay

Designed and typeset by Textype Typesetters, Cambridge
Printed and bound in China by Leo Paper Products

# Contents

# Introduction

The excitement of opening presents starts when, as small children, we are shown how to tear off the paper that covers a gift. It doesn't take long to learn, and that sense of anticipation of what lies inside a package remains with us all our lives. Elaborate packaging need not be expensive and can contain a relatively simple gift or perhaps a cheque. And sometimes it's fun to tease by using a recycled box quite unrelated to the gift within: thus the receiver may unwrap the paper to discover a box that apparently contains an iron or a cut-glass vase, only to find, say, a camera within!

In this book I offer you many ideas for presenting your gifts: I show you how to deal with those hard-to-pack shapes, I give you ideas for novelty packaging that you might like to keep, I suggest some uses for recycled materials, and describe ways to achieve unusual but inexpensive effects. Every project has clear step-by-step instructions, and templates are included, as well as lots of ideas for co-ordinated gift cards.

Many imaginative craft techniques have been employed: some of these will be familiar, though perhaps used in different styles, others will give you the opportunity to try new projects at a manageable size.

There is packaging for all occasions, including instructions for hand-made carrier bags, boxes of various shapes, hints on how to achieve neat folds and closures, as well as interesting ideas with ribbons. Many of the projects are suitable for children to tackle – and at the same time neatly demonstrate how important it is to reward special efforts with the words 'thank you'.

A whole range of exciting theme packages is covered, any of which may be chosen to reflect the recipient's favourite hobby or to suit the occasion; and although the projects are grouped in chapters, the techniques are so versatile that you can adapt them for the appropriate celebration. There are also dozens of handy tips scattered throughout the book.

I very much hope that these pages will inspire you to expand the various techniques and create your own versions, whether you are a novice or have experience, and that you will take pleasure in personalizing them. Lots of materials can be found around the house, but by developing an eye for collecting interesting bits and pieces when you are out and about, you will never be short of unique ideas. I call my collection 'Maybe sometime'. My family has laughed at me for years, for on birthdays, special occasions and at Christmas I save the beautiful paper, ribbons and boxes for future use . . . and they do get used.

I urge you to read through the book first, and enjoy its pages – and then let the creativity flow!

# IT'S A WRAP!

Wrappings need not be expensive – though we are probably all guilty at some time or other of buying paper we just can't resist, knowing how much pleasure it will give to others. The diverse selection of papers on the opposite page gives some idea of the range of coverings that are available. Books containing tear-out gift wrap featuring fabric designs or patchwork are a gift in themselves, and if to these we add all the papers which have been created specially for this book, we are spoiled for choice.

Ready-printed gift wrap that we purchase off the shop shelf comes in a huge variety of designs and colours, often with co-ordinated ribbon and gift cards. Generally speaking, cheaper paper is thinner, making it harder to get crisp folds, and it sometimes tears on the corners before the parcel is packed. Paper that is too thick is equally frustrating, as it springs wilfully apart before sticky tape can be applied. Better quality wrapping paper does not mark as easily as inexpensive versions. With experience you will learn to choose wisely – but it is worth noting that presents for children need thinner paper so that they can rip it off and get their presents out as quickly as possible!

Crêpe paper can be found in both bright and pastel colours, sometimes reversible, as well as in coloured metallics, gold and silver. It is very useful for wrapping cylindrical gifts as it stretches slightly, but it can repel some types of sticky tape.

Foils come in various colours, printed, bonded to paper, or double-sided gold and silver. Try using them with tissue paper to get the juxtaposition of matt and shiny.

Tissue paper is available in a huge range of colours and is one of my favourites. Double sheets give dense colour and a luxurious feel – used plain they make a wonderful background for elaborate ribbons and bows. They can be painted or printed, or they may be combined, one piece overlapping another, to make yet further shades. Used sheets can be cut into strips for packaging fragile gifts.

Brown paper is a useful base for printing, stamping, stencilling and marbling. It is very tough, and looks particularly good when combined with raffia or rough parcel string.

Hand-made paper is so beautiful that it really is essential to learn how to fasten up a parcel without using sticky tape. The splendid piece of hand-made and printed fish paper opposite is now on its third owner! Petals, silk threads and leaves can all be incorporated into hand-made papers.

Flower-shop paper is inexpensive, and is often the run-on used to clean the rollers after textile printing; it therefore comes in a wide variety of wild designs. Your friendly florist may be willing to sell sheets for a small fee; likewise he may be able to provide cellophane.

Butcher's paper is also very cheap, and is particularly useful for printing and for underwrapping where there might be show-through. It tears easily, so makes good torn paper stencils.

**TIP:**
In an ideal world we would all be able to store paper flat: in practice, rolling it around a tube (from the carpet shop, cut to size) will take up less room. Wrap a band of scrap paper around the roll, and close with sticky tape.

**TIP:**
Sometimes it is easier to paint or print the paper flat, at other times after it has been folded around the present.

**TIP:**
Try tinting paper with cold dye colours, or 'age' it with cold tea.

**TIP:**
Recycle paper by pressing it with a cool dry iron.

**TIP:**
All paper has a grain and will tear more easily in one direction. Sometimes the grain can be seen with the naked eye. It is just as well to practise on test scraps.

**TIP:**
Take a cardboard tube with you when shopping for papers: you can roll them round it, and this will protect them on your journey home.

**TIP:**
Collect white shoe boxes in which to store your creative odds and ends. Ask your friends to save them too. Make decorative labels, or cover them in used gift wrap.

**TIP:**

When cutting a motif from card, trim roughly around the shape before working on the drawn line.

**TIP:**

Look in charity outlets for beads and novelty items, and try toy shops for stickers and tiny objects. Jumble and boot sales can yield all manner of delights.

Sugar paper is a little too thick for wrapping, but its bright colours make it useful for decoration. It too can be printed, stencilled and embossed.

Different fabrics make highly effective gift wrapping: for instance, the Japanese often wrap gifts in antique kimono silk; and traditionally, packages from India come sewn into calico. Net, lace, silk and velvet all evoke different moods.

For fragile gifts, plastic bubblewrap can be sprayed with car paint and then stitched into pouches.

Designer's layout and tracing paper can be painted with patterns and sprayed. And of course, if you are really desperate there is always newspaper (pink, white or yellow) which can be sprayed, stencilled and printed.

## ADORNMENTS

Once I have wrapped all my Christmas presents, I then collect together the ribbons and 'maybe someday' and have the most wonderful time adorning them and making the gift tags. I colour co-ordinate my cards, the gifts and the Christmas tree so that the presents are part of the display. The picture opposite gives some idea of the many decorative items which appear in this book, as well as some more to whet your appetite.

Stationer's dots come in all sizes: colour them with felt-tip pens, or try eyelets and studs in leather, suede or felt. There is also a huge variety of beads and many ways to use them, either alone, or with sequins and buttons, sisha mirrors and tiny trinkets.

Paint comes in many guises, too: sten-cil, poster, fabric, car and craft spray. These may be applied with sponges, paint and stencil brushes, or combined with foiling, sparkle fragments, emboss-ing and stencilling and stamping. Use pretty feathers, lace and trinkets and embroidery threads.

Don't forget that fabrics also have a place in gift wrapping: they can be cut into strips and used as ribbons, or sewn around a present; leave the tail end of the thread tied in a bow, for easy opening. And you will see that fur fabric and towelling make an appearance in this book, and flowers too.

# 1 Tools, Materials and Techniques

## TOOLS OF THE TRADE

Gift wrapping is a creative activity, but using the right tools always makes the job easier.

### Cutting and measuring

- A self-healing cutting mat printed with a grid is a good investment for all types of craft work. However, you can also use a vinyl tile or piece of thick cardboard for cutting on.
- A steel ruler is ideal for ruling and cutting against.
- Measure curves with a tape measure, holding it on edge when checking a curved line.
- It is safer and more accurate to work with a sharp craft knife, preferably with snap-off blades which are quick and easy. Use a scalpel if you are familiar with one.
- Keep one pair of scissors for cutting paper, and another pair for fabric. Small embroidery scissors are best for intricate shapes, though pinking and deckle scissors will give an instant decorative finish.
- Hole punches come in many different designs and create well defined cut-out shapes.
- A stapler is useful for joining card.
- A set square is invaluable for measuring accurate corners.

## Adhesives

- Motifs can be attached in a variety of ways, but double-sided sticky tape gives a better finish for closing packages as it can be hidden under folds.
- Magic tape is useful for holding paper in place temporarily, but coloured sticky tape makes for a more decorative finish. Using tape held in a dispenser makes the job a lot easier.
- Spray glue – which should be used in a spray booth – is most effective for sticking paper to paper.
- PVA or rubber-based glues will mark fabric, so leave these to dry slightly before use. Watered-down PVA can be used to strengthen paper. There is less chance of a mishap if the PVA is poured into the lid from a cardboard tube or palette. Use an orange stick or small spreader to apply and handle tiny pieces with tweezers.

**TIP:**
To prevent the surrounding furnishings getting sticky with glue drift, make yourself a spray booth from a large cardboard box, with an old telephone directory as a base. Each time you use the spray glue, turn over a page so that next time you will have a clean page.

**TIP:**
All-purpose clear adhesive will stick metal, plastic and glass and now comes in gel form which does not 'string'.

**TIP:**

If recycled, ironed ribbons still have creases, cut off and save the good areas and slip them through the knot of a bow, just before pulling it tight.

**TIP:**

Store ribbons by winding them onto a gift-wrap or kitchen-roll tube.

Bottom left: Step 1 – Form two loops.
Bottom right: Step 2 – Tie the loops together.

## ALL TIED UP

Bows and ribbons tumbling in curls on a gift seem to add a frivolous note, but they can also add style to a simple presentation, or provide the perfect finishing touch for an elaborate creation. Try combining several widths and types of ribbon: say, a wide wire-edged velvet and a narrow satin arrangement, or several different types of metallic silver, including tinsel, or even a mixture of garden string and raffia for a gardener. How about a leather thong or a strip of leather with punched eyelets for motor-cycle fans? Or brightly coloured string gathered from the beach with a pebble or shell attached? Add baubles, charms, flowers (fresh, paper or silk), dried fruit, wrapped sweets or ready-made rosettes, and you will begin to see some of the exciting possibilities.

Large, brightly coloured plastic bags can be cut into lengths, paper can be sliced into strips, and net and organza cut across the grain (so that it will not fray). Crepe paper frilled at the edges looks pretty with lace, and narrow strips

of paper can be combined and twisted or plaited. On page 28 we demonstrate how to make cord both by hand and with a sewing machine.

A bow does not have to be placed in the exact centre of a package: try putting the ribbon around the sides of the box, with the bow on top and ribbons cascading down the front and back. Make a crossover high on the front, or just run a simple band around the package. Wrap ribbon around the corners of a box, or use a sumptuous ribbon tied into a simple knot.

Don't neglect the ends of ribbons – add stars and stickies, or cut them in a 'v' shape, or at 45 degrees or straight. The way to curl ribbon is to pull it over the blade of a closed pair of scissors.

### Basic bow

1. Cut a length of ribbon. Find the centre and form two loops on either side.
2. Tie the two loops together in a bow. Trim the ends.

**TIP:**

It is more economical to buy ribbon on a roll than by the metre (yard).

## START HERE

Measurements are not provided for all the projects, as all gifts will be different sizes; however, it is important to follow either metric or imperial as each will make up to a different size – thus they are not interchangeable.

I strongly advise you to read through the introductory pages of the book before starting on any of the projects. As you browse through the rest of the book, glance at the tips, for they are all there to make gift wrapping a pleasure.

## Basic wrapping

Give yourself enough time to present gifts with impact. We devote a lot of thought to the pleasure our gifts will give someone special, but we often leave the packaging to the last minute, and this is a pity, as making the coverings can be as much fun as shopping for the presents. The key to successful gift wrapping is to have a good store of boxes in which to pack items. It is also much easier if the paper is cut to size, as this avoids lumpy areas of excess paper around the gift. Sometimes the package needs to be lined with white paper in order to prevent showthrough.

Always work in good light, and clear a space so that there is enough room to work. Before starting, assemble all the components: gift, box, wrapping paper, cutting board, sticky tape, scissors, craft knife, ribbons and so on. If necessary, open a window for ventilation.

1. Measure the box with a tape measure all the way round and half way down the sides. In general, square boxes are easier to wrap if the paper finishes half way down the sides; flatter boxes are more manageable if the paper ends at the base. Remembering the old adage 'measure twice, cut once', cut the paper to size.

Step 1 – Measure the box in two directions.

Step 2 – Apply double-sided sticky tape.

**TIP:**
Before starting, cut some pieces of sticky tape and 'park' them on the edge of the cutting board or the table, slightly away from where you are working.

**TIP:**
It's much easier to make a cylinder or gift bag around a former such as a used biscuit tube or box.

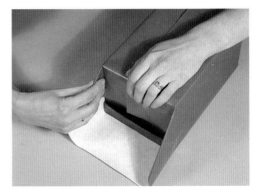

2. With the right side of the paper on the table, fold in the overlap of about 2.5cm (1in) and attach a piece of double-sided sticky tape. Place the gift face down in the centre, and pull up the sides of the paper, folding in an overlap of about 2.5cm (1in). To close, centre the overlap fold and stick.

3. Crease the folds with a finger and thumb. Centre the box inside the paper, and at one end fold a corner of the paper against the box as shown. Repeat and crease, making sure your fingers push the paper right into the corners.

4. Fold in the side flaps, keeping the corners sharp, and after folding in the apex of the point, attach sticky tape and close. Repeat for the other side.

**TIP:**
Don't forget that when you need a third hand, you can temporarily hold things in place with a piece of low-tack masking tape or BluTac.

Top left: Step 3 – Fold in side flaps.

Left: Step 4 – Attach sticky tape.

**TIP:**
When painting or writing on a box, steady your hand by resting it on another box of about the same height.

**TIP:**
Keep handy a clean, flat, 5–7cm (2–3in) stone as a weight to stop papers sliding off the table while you measure and cut.

## BASIC BOXES

Using a box is the key to successful gift wrapping, and sometimes a purpose-made box provides the perfect presentation. Here we provide templates and instructions for making a variety of boxes, one to suit most occasions. For custom-made boxes, measure the height and width of the present, and follow the instructions for making a box with a separate lid, adapting the dimensions to fit. The larger the box, the heavier the card you should use.

### Cube box with a hinged lid

Top: Step 3 – Attaching double-sided sticky tape.

Bottom: Close cushion box with a bow.

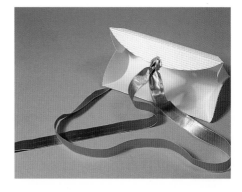

This box is approximately 10cm (4in).

*YOU WILL NEED:*

- Card, not less than 216g (7.6oz) in weight, 45cm×31cm (18in×12½in)
- H pencil
- Cutting mat
- Steel rule
- Sharp craft knife
- Double-sided sticky tape

1. Enlarge the template on page 91 by 200 per cent: using it as a guide, lightly draw the long outline, 42cm (16½in). Note that to allow the box to close, the lid should be made a fraction larger than the box sides and base. Draw the lid, base and tabs. The dashed lines are guides for scoring (always on the outside) and folding, the continuous line is the cutting line.

2. Score the dashed lines, using the back of the craft knife, taking care not to press too heavily. Using a steel rule, cut out the box. Follow the four cut line guides for the lid section.

3. Attach strips of double-sided sticky tape to the tabs. Fold along the score lines, pinching with thumb and fingers to get crisp corners. Attach the tab on the longest side first, making up the base next. Fold in the corners of the lid and stick.

### Cushion box with a wrap-over lid

This box is approximately 15cm×8cm (6in×3in).

*YOU WILL NEED*

- Corrugated card 20sq cm (8sq in)
- Tracing paper
- Cutting mat
- Steel rule
- Craft knife
- Alternative sticky seal or ribbon
- Hole punch

1. Trace the template on page 90 and transfer it to the back of the card, following the instructions for the cube box. The grain should run across the cushion. Cut out and score the fold lines, on the outside, taking care not to cut too deeply. Punch a hole in the centre of the flap and thread a length of ribbon through, so that one half has a longer tail: this will wrap around the cushion. Fold in the ends first, then gently roll into shape. Pop in your present and seal the flap!

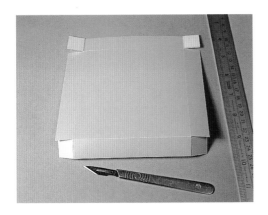

## Box with separate lid

This box is approximately 12cm×5cm deep (4¾in×2in).

*YOU WILL NEED*

◆ Card 50cm×25cm (20in×10in)
◆ Cutting mat
◆ Craft knife
◆ Steel rule
◆ Double-sided sticky tape

1. Enlarge the template on page 93 by 200 per cent, noting that the lid is slightly larger than the box. Draw the lid, then the base, making the sides deeper. Score on the dashed lines and cut out. Then follow the instructions for the cube box and lid.

Far left: Folding in the corners of the lid.

**TIP:**
When marking always use a sharp pencil, non-stop propelling pencils are handy as they do not need sharpening.

**TIP:**
Tracing paper and thin card will be needed for making templates.

Step 1 – Fold towards the centre.

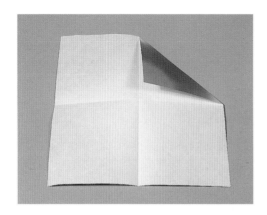

Step 2 – All four corners towards the centre.

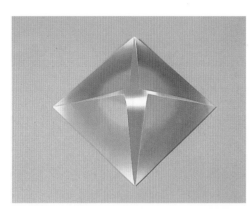

Step 3 – Fold the points under.

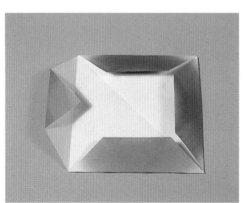

**TIP:**
To help you to understand the technique, make a practice box from paper with lines or printing on one side only. The final box should be made from paper with colour or printing on both sides.

# ORIGAMI BOX

The Japanese art of paper folding can be useful for creating hand-made boxes. It is best to use strong paper, although painting the finished box with several coats of a mixture of PVA glue and water will make it very durable. A sheet of paper 15cm×15cm (6in×6in) will make a finished box measuring 5.5cm (2¼in). To make a lid, cut the paper .05cm (¹⁄₁₆in) larger. It is essential to start with an accurate square of paper.

*METHOD*

1. For the box and lid, cut two squares. Take the smaller square and make creased guide lines by folding the paper edge to edge and side to side. Run your fingers along the folds to make a crease.

2. Fold each of the four corners towards the centre mark.

3. Fold all the points under so that they meet the inner edge.

4. Turn over and make two vertical folds so that the sides meet in the centre.

5. Make a diagonal guide fold across each corner. Lift up and separate the edges, then fold the triangle corner between the top side layer and the bottom layer. Repeat on all the corners.

6. With both hands, slip your fingers into the centre slot and gently pull to each side, forming a box shape with your finger and thumb. Pinch the sides to make sharp creases. Repeat with the larger square to make the lid.

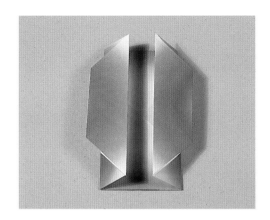

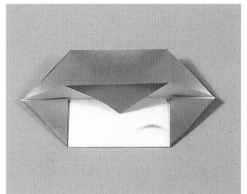

Far left: Step 4 – Two vertical folds.

Left: Step 5(i) – Diagonal guide folds.

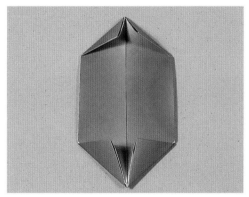

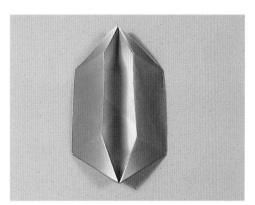

Far left: Step 5(ii) – Fold between layers.

Left: Step 6 – Open to form a square.

# FOLDED PAPER, LACED AND TAPED BOXES

Right: Folded paper box.

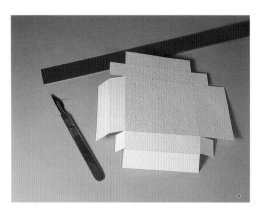

Here are some more ways to make decorative boxes. The folded, hand-made paper box has dried flowers added, painted with PVA glue, which strengthens the paper. The laced card made from corrugated plastic has ribbons to hold the sides together. Decorative tape is used to finish the corners on our pretty green box. Always make box lids 2mm (⅛in) larger overall.

## Folded box and lid

This box is approximately 8cm (3¼in).

*YOU WILL NEED*

- 2 sheets of hand-made paper 38cm×28cm (15in×11in)
- Tracing paper
- Ruler
- Sharp pencil
- Craft knife
- Double-sided sticky tape

1. Enlarge the design on page 93 by 150 per cent and transfer to the right side of the paper. Cut along the outside lines and score on the dotted lines. Cut away the corner squares as shown in the diagram. Cut along the line to the four corners. Stick four narrow strips of double-sided sticky tape along the edges on the wrong side.

2. Fold along the score lines, using the bevelled edge of a clean ruler to make a sharp fold. Erase the pencil guide lines. Remove the protective covering from the sticky tape from two opposite sides, and fold in. Repeat on the other two sides, encasing the flaps with the double-sided sticky tape.

## Laced plastic card box

This box measures 11.5cm×6.5cm (4½in×2½in)

*YOU WILL NEED*

- Piece of fluted plastic card 23cm×18cm (9in×7in)
- Tracing paper
- Sharp craft knife
- Ruler
- Hole punch
- Double-sided sticky tape
- 2m (2yd) narrow ribbon

**TIP:**
Double sided sticky pads are marvellous for attaching all sorts of odd shapes to paper and fabric.

Far right: Box with laced sides.

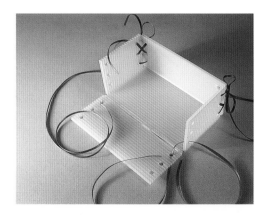

1.  Trace the template on page 92 and attach it to the plastic card with a couple of pieces of double-sided sticky tape. Cut along the outside edges, taking a small notch out of each corner, so that the short sides will fold neatly. Mark and punch holes as showing. The long sides are scored on the inside, the short sides on the outside.

2.  Cut the ribbon into four pieces. Starting on the inside base, thread the ribbon through two holes, crossing them before threading through the next two holes. Finish with a bow. Repeat for the other three sides.

## Box with taped corners

This box is 11.5cm×6.5cm (4½in× 2½in)

*YOU WILL NEED*

- ◆ Piece of card 23cm×18cm (9in×7in)
- ◆ Tracing paper
- ◆ Sharp craft knife
- ◆ Ruler
- ◆ Pencil
- ◆ Decorative sticky tape 2.5cm (1in)

Trace the template on page 92 and, omitting the 'notched' corners, transfer to the wrong side of the card. Cut along the outside edges and score on the right side, as shown. Draw a light guideline 12mm (½in) on one side of each corner. We used the end of a tissue box as a 'former' to help hold the box firm while the sides were taped. Cut strips of adhesive tape to fit the corners of the box, adding extra for folding over. Place the box on the former and attach the

tape, folding in the excess. To make a lid, reduce the depth of the sides and make the top slightly larger.

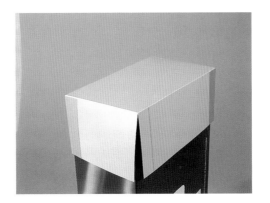

Box with taped corners.

**TIP:**
Remember, everyone has a use for an eraser at some time or other!

## WRAPPING DIFFICULT SHAPES

**TIP:**
Use low tack masking tape to temporarily hold paper or fabric in place while they are being worked on.

### Wrapping a sphere

When time is short and there is no handy box in which to pack a round gift – wrap it! Fabric is easier to manipulate than paper, and net is inexpensive and comes in many colours, so be lavish.

Cut a good size square of net – we used 50cm (20in) – and place the gift in the centre. Make small pleats all the way round, holding them in place with masking tape, then tie with a length of yarn. From a contrasting colour net, cut a wide length about a metre (3¼ft) long, and tie in an extravagant bow.

### Wrapping a tube

A cylinder can always be made into a faux cracker by tying ribbons at each end. However, an elegant solution would be to wrap the tube diagonally and finish with a beautiful ribbon.

Cut the wrapping paper into a square with the sides the same length as the tube. Place the centre of the tube on one corner and commence wrapping diagonally. Tie a large bow.

**TIP:** A compass will ensure an accurate circle, less chancy than drawing round a jam jar.

Wrapping a sphere.

## Covering a box

Recycle a shoe box by covering it in gift wrap, then simply add a decorative bow.

1. Place the shoe box in the middle of a sheet of paper and draw around the base; then tip the box on its sides, measuring all four. You should have a pattern similar to page 92. Add turnings of about 1cm (½in) on all edges. Cut out the shape.

Above: Wrapping a tube diagonally.
Left: Covering a box.

2. Spray glue (using the spray booth) on the wrong side of the paper. Put the box in the centre and smooth up the sides, folding in the top and side overlaps. Cut off the side overlaps at each end, and cut into the corners to help them to lie flat. Fold up the ends and smooth flat, tucking in the top overlaps. Make the lid in the same way.

# 2 Births and Birthdays

From childhood we all appreciate a beautifully packed gift on our birthday. The following pages will inspire you to catch the mood of the celebration.

# STICK 'EM UP!

Sometimes when you are in a hurry, great effects can be achieved by simply attaching one or two amusing little gimmicks to a package. Some of these ideas will produce a giggle both for you and your friends.

*YOU WILL NEED*

- Wrapping papers
- A selection of coloured buttons or
- Small feathers or
- Zip
- Sticky pad
- PVA glue
- Double-sided sticky tape
- Small piece of yellow card
- Small piece of orange card

*METHOD*

1. The parcels are wrapped in the usual way, except for the buttons version which is in reverse, making a feature of the folded edge along the top. Attach the double-sided sticky tape away from the fold, so that it will become more obvious, giving the impression of a buttoned garment. Cut a sticky pad into small pieces and apply one piece to the back of each button, then peel off the backing paper and put them on the fold.

2. Thin strips of double-sided sticky tape have been used to attach the zip. Centre, and then press the sides of the zip onto the gift wrap, starting at one end, gently pressing your fingers along the length.

3. A white lining paper has been used under a thick grade, coloured tracing paper on the feather package. The feathers are held in place with a little dab of PVA glue.

Make the gift tag by folding a diamond-shape card in half: this will give you a triangle. Tear a small piece of tissue paper into a similar shape, attach with spray glue and add a button using a tiny triangle of sticky pad. The feathers on the orange gift tag appear to be in a tall vase, made from a square wooden bead.

Above: Step 1.

Bottom: Step 2.

**TIP:**
To cut narrow strips of sticky tape, attach the required length to the cutting board and using the grid, cut against a steel rule with a sharp craft knife. Don't leave them in place overnight as the sticky tape might lift off the printed grid.

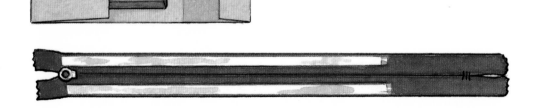

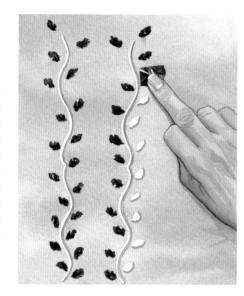

## FOILING VINES

Petty foiled garlands complement hand-made cords and tassels. The tassels can be saved and used on key rings or light pulls. Instructions for a tassel are on page 73, and we show you how to make quick cord. The foil is applied to special pressure-sensitive adhesive after it has dried. Once you start to play with this technique it is hard to stop, so make cards or even decorate your clothes with unique embellishments.

Right: Step 2.
Far right: Step 3.
Below: Step 4.

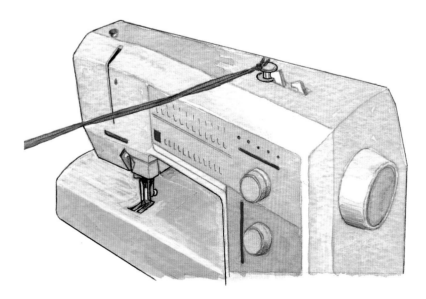

### YOU WILL NEED

- Special pressure-sensitive adhesive
- Foils in pink and green
- Wrapping paper
- Piece of card for tassel and template
- Scissors
- Masking tape
- Sticky tape
- Embroidery yarns or crochet thread
- Optional, sewing machine and bobbin
- Optional, two pencils

### METHOD

1. Measure the box to be wrapped and, using a sharp pencil, lightly mark the area which will be on the top of the package. Trace the template stem and transfer to a piece of card (see page 43). Cut out on the curved line.

2. Using a small piece of masking tape on each corner to hold the paper still, centre and draw the stem line about 2.5cm (1in) from the edge. Add the little 'flowers'. Read the product instructions, then paint over the line with the pressure-sensitive adhesive. Leave to dry.

3. When the adhesive is dry, cut a small piece of pink foil and, with the colour side uppermost, put onto the adhesive and gently rub with your finger. When all the flowers are finished, add the next colour to the stem. Wrap the parcel.

4. Make the cord by cutting several lengths of embroidery thread three times longer than the length required, and tie a knot at each end. Attach one end to the bobbin by threading a polyester thread through the little hole and knotting it into the yarn. Put the bobbin onto the sewing machine winder and, keeping the yarns taut, press the machine foot to wind the bobbin. Distribute the twist evenly by smoothing your fingers along whilst winding. When it seems tight enough, pinch the centre between finger and thumb, and with the other hand bring the two ends together. The cord will rapidly double up. Cut the ends even and attach to the tassel.

Vine template

**TIP:**

Cord can also be made by inserting a pencil into each end and two people, keeping the yarns taut, twisting in opposite directions. Children love this project.

# SOFT 'N SQUASHY

It is always a challenge to disguise soft and squashy gifts such as socks and scarves, but you can re-use a coffee tin with a plastic lid by covering it with fabric, paper or gift wrap and colouring the lid with spray paint. Here we have used a paper reminiscent of motor-racing flags, and have painted the lid red. The other cylinder has been wrapped to look like a candle.

*YOU WILL NEED*

- A clean tin with a snap-on plastic lid
- Gift wrap or fabric
- Aerosol car paint
- Double-sided sticky tape or glue
- Scissors
- Ruler
- Tape measure
- An old salt or crisp cylinder
- Black paper
- White stationery dots or black-spotted gift wrap
- A small piece of orange or red paper

*METHOD*

1. Wash and dry the lid thoroughly. Using a spray booth (page 11), shake well and then point the nozzle at the lid from a distance of about 25cm (10in) and spray in short bursts until it is evenly covered. Leave to dry.

2. Measure around the tin and from top to bottom. Cut the paper or fabric to fit, with an overlap of about 1cm (½in) along the short edge. If the paper has a pattern, mark the top and overlap edge at one end. Cut

a narrow length of double-sided sticky tape and attach to the short (overlap) edge.

3. Mark a vertical straight guideline where the join will start, and put a short length of double-sided tape along it. Cut narrow strips of double-sided tape and attach around the top and base of the tin. Peel off the protective cover from the sticky tape on the tin and, starting from the guideline, carefully roll the paper around the tin. Finally, strip off the sticky tape cover and close the join.

4. For the candle: either use black paper and attach stationer's dots, or buy bold wrapping paper. The paper does not need to be folded at the base or top. Follow step 2, then put the present in the tube and close the top. Cut a circle to fit the top of the cylinder and attach it with glue. Trace the flame template on page 91 and cut the flame from orange or red paper and stick on the top.

**TIP:**
Be sure to check that there are no sharp edges around the rim of the tin.

**TIP:**
Use blue or white tack to hold the tape in place while measuring.

Step 3.

**TIP:**
Use a wrapped cylinder as a back support for flat cut-out shapes, such as a Christmas tree, held in place with sticky pads.

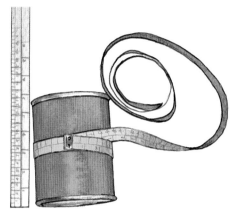

Step 2.

**TIP:**
Wash the stencil
and brushes in
washing-up liquid,
and dry well.
Check they are
dry before re-
using. Put the lids
on the pots – the
sealing layer will
form again.

**TIP:**
A fresh rose could
be used.

# STENCILLING

Stencilling is a fun and quick way to make patterns on both gift wrap and cards. However, it is addictive, so be warned! Here we have started simply with one stencil, blue and red dry stencil paint, and two brushes. Although it is an easy procedure, take the time to practise the technique on a spare piece of the same paper, and to familiarize yourself with the stencil.

*YOU WILL NEED*

- Good quality, plain gift wrap to fit the package
- Purchased stencil
- Two colours dry stencil paint
- Two stencil brushes
- Kitchen-roll paper
- Low-tack sticky tape
- Double-sided sticky tape
- Washing-up liquid
- Ribbons, rose and stick-on heart to decorate

*METHOD*

1. Cut the gift wrap to fit the package, and lightly mark where the top, sides and folded area will fall. Work out where the stencil will give most impact, and mark with pencil register dots. Tape the corners of the paper to a flat surface. Cover the stencil hanging hole with masking tape. Lightly tape the stencil to the first area to be painted.

2. Following the manufacturer's instructions, peel off the covering from the top of the paints. Select one colour (we used red in the little heart shapes) and rub the brush in the paint, dusting off the residue on a piece of kitchen paper. Lightly paint with a dabbing or swirling circular action, building up the colour by using pressure rather than more paint. To get a sharp, clean image, be sure to cover the edges.

3. Paint a little red in the other shapes and then, using a clean brush, repeat adding blue to the remaining apertures, and in some areas combining the two colours. Cover the painted parts with a piece of clean paper, and continue until the gift wrap is decorated. Leave to dry – be guided by your trial piece as to when it will be safe to wrap the package.

We expanded on the romantic theme of hearts with a red silk rose, and attached loops of narrow ribbon and a simple bow, held in place with a red sticky heart.

Right: Step 2.
Far right: Step 3.

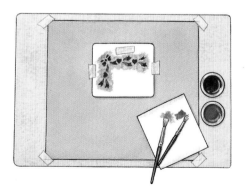

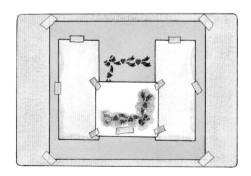

## TIP:

Any fabric can be used for this technique, a gift of patchwork fabrics for a quilter could be wrapped in one of the pieces and the sisha omitted.

# VELVET AND SISHA MIRRORS

An unusual and luxurious presentation for a glamorous friend perhaps, or one who enjoys textiles. We have combined velvet and sisha mirrors, which are normally attached with buttonhole stitch, but for speed we have glued them in place, with glitter contour paint covering the edges. The parcel is closed not with sticky tape, but by sewing a simple running stitch so that it can be opened by untying the bows at each end and pulling out the thread.

*YOU WILL NEED*

- An off-cut of velvet to fit the parcel
- Pins
- Embroidery needle
- Silver embroidery thread
- Sisha mirrors
- All-purpose glue
- Silver glitter contour paint
- Pinking shears
- Organza ribbon, narrow ribbon and two droplets

*METHOD*

1.  To avoid fraying, use pinking shears to cut the fabric to size. Fold the

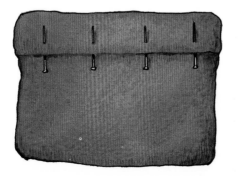

Step 1.

material around the package, with a folded edge opening on top. Hold the creases in place with plenty of pins.

2.  Thread a length of silver embroidery yarn, enough to sew across the parcel leaving a tail of about 10cm (4in), and sew just above the fold. Leave the tails without knots. Sew the side folds in the same way but with a knot at one end, finishing sewing on the top corner. Tie the ends of the embroidery thread in a little bow.

3.  Find the top centre of the package and, using a ruler and an empty biro or your nail, mark a line to each corner. This should make a dent in the velvet which will show as a guide. Squeeze some glue into a paint palette and, using tweezers to hold the sisha mirrors, spread a little glue on the backs. Position the mirrors and leave to dry.

4.  Following the manufacturer's instructions, squeeze the contour paint around the mirrors and leave to dry for an hour or so, when the glitter will start to show.

Decorate with a lavish arrangement of two widths of organza ribbon and two glass droplets. Make the basic bow (page 12) and add loops of the narrower ribbon, held on the reverse with a stitch or dab of glue. Sew on the two droplets and attach the bow with a sticky pad.

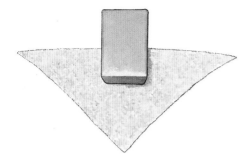

# BABY TALK

Here's a fun way to give a gift to a new baby – in a towelling or face-cloth cover. First wrap the present in the traditional colours of pink for a girl or blue for a boy. Depending on the size of the package, you could use a hand towel, towelling yardage or a face-cloth.

## *YOU WILL NEED*

- ◆ Tissue paper in either pink or blue (or both!)
- ◆ Towelling fabric
- ◆ Sticky tape
- ◆ A nappy safety pin
- ◆ Ribbons to co-ordinate with the parcel
- ◆ Optional: sewing maching and thread

## *METHOD*

1. Following the general wrapping instructions on page 14, prepare the package in the appropriate colour tissue paper. Use a spare piece of paper to measure the size of triangle needed to fit half the package, leaving the top showing. Cut the towelling into a triangle shape and machine-sew a zig-zag stitch around the edges. This could be in a colour co-ordinated thread.

2. Whether you are using a towel, face-cloth or fabric, fold the material into a triangle shape so that it resembles a nappy (diaper), and where the three corners meet, close with a nappy pin. Tuck the 'leg' openings inside the gap at each side. Tie the ribbons around the gift so that they will show above the 'nappy'.

Using a small triangle of terry towelling, the theme can also be adapted for birth cards, or gift tags. Lightly hold the card in place with masking tape on each corner, then measure and rule a faint line an equal distance around the card. Using the wrong side of a bevel-edge ruler, draw a border in felt-tip pen. Measure diagonally from each corner and mark an X in the centre, then attach the 'nappy' using double-sided sticky tape.

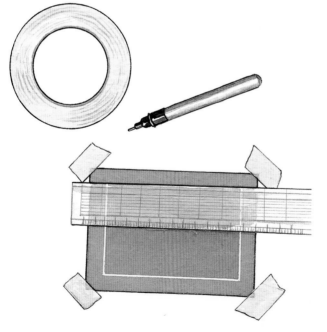

Top left: Step 1.
Middle left:Step 2.
Bottom left: Measuring and drawing a border line.

## MAKE YOUR MARK WITH STAMPING

Ready-made stamps can be used in a variety of creative ways, printing on card, paper and fabric. Here, just two purchased stamps will provide many decorative ideas for packaging. To add interest, the stamps can be washed and re-used on different colour pads.

### YOU WILL NEED

- ◆ Two purchased stamps (one border, one icon)
- ◆ Rainbow ink-pad
- ◆ Various papers including brown
- ◆ Co-ordinated cards
- ◆ Scissors
- ◆ Sticky tape
- ◆ Spray glue
- ◆ Raffia

### METHOD

1. Cut the paper to fit the gift box. On the right side, in the centre, lightly draw a size guideline for the top of the box. Draw the same size guideline on a spare piece of paper, and check that the border stamp will fit neatly. Practise, varying the pressure when inking the stamp and printing on the paper.

2. When you have decided on the design, print the centre panel, continuing, if you wish, to cover the whole sheet of paper. Be sure the ink is dry before wrapping the parcel.

3. Make co-ordinated greetings and gift tags by printing directly onto card or torn paper. It is also an ideal opportunity to have fun by very quickly making a stock of cards, thus ensuring you will never be caught out with an unexpected birthday! Check that you have envelopes to fit before cutting the cards. Personalize your greetings by using the stamps on the envelopes, too.

As our stamps have an ethnic flavour we have used raffia to finish off the packages. A turk's head knot was worked on the larger parcel, with the raffia ends wrapped around and finished at the back with sticky tape. Red raffia was used knotted, and then some short extra pieces added under another knot.

**TIP:**
String can be made by cutting from the length of crepe paper and then twisting by hand, or try cutting across the width and frilling the edges between your fingers.

**TIP:**
It is not possible to print on paper which has a shiny surface – the ink will never dry! Always check on a scrap before starting the project.

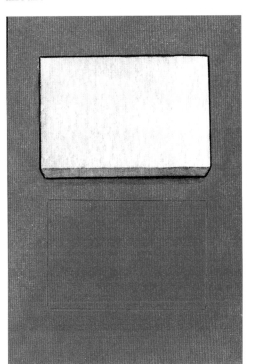

Left: Step 1.

# 3 Occasions

The yearly calendar is dotted with red letter days, from Valentines to Golden Weddings. Make yours a gift to remember.

# DUCKING AND DIVING AT EASTERTIME

Mother duck template.

The delightful sight of a mother duck taking her young for a walk can be seen every spring in parks and around ponds everywhere. Our ducks are dressed up in their best with blue-and-white checked ribbons around their necks. The template can be reduced or enlarged for many other uses, too.

## YOU WILL NEED

- ◆ Tracing paper
- ◆ B lead pencil
- ◆ Sharp pencil
- ◆ Paper scissors
- ◆ Narrow blue-and-white checked ribbon
- ◆ PVA glue
- ◆ White card
- ◆ Yellow wrapping paper

## METHOD

1. Wrap the gift following the guidelines on page 14. For the mother duck, trace out the template on this page. The young ducks can be used from the template on page 89. To transfer the outlines to white card, first scribble on the wrong side of the tracing using a soft B pencil. Hold the pencil flat. Put the tracing on a piece of white card and hold in place with masking tape. Draw over the outline with a sharp pencil.

2. Cut out the ducks and through the wing shape using a sharp craft knife. Arrange them on the front of the parcel, marking faint pencil dots as guidelines. Turn the duck shapes over and glue the body backs, taking care not to make the wings sticky.

Attach them to the package and with the tip of a craft knife lift the wings up. Draw the features in pen or leave them blank. Glue the checked ribbon bands and bows on the ducks' necks. Add some extra checked ribbon if you wish.

We repeated the duck outline on the gift tag, having reduced it on the photocopier.

Step 1.

Step 2.

# MOVING DAY

Sure to raise a smile on moving day, this package uses dolls' house brick paper, here converted into wrapping paper, with a roof incorporated onto the package. A front door, windows and greenery add to the fun; the roof is attached last. The design will work better with a tall gift, so take that into consideration when shopping!

*YOU WILL NEED*

- ◆ Dolls' house brick paper
- ◆ Grey or black card
- ◆ Small pieces of white, yellow and red card or paper
- ◆ Ruler
- ◆ Black or silver marker
- ◆ Craft knife
- ◆ Double-sided sticky tape
- ◆ PVA glue
- ◆ Scissors

*METHOD*

1. Cut the dolls' house brick paper to size, and wrap the package as shown on page 14. For each window cut a wide 'T' shape of white card or paper for the window and sill, and two yellow square 'panes'. Cut a white rectangle with a semicircle for the fanlight, make the front door from red card or paper, and use a tiny piece of gold for the letterbox. Assemble and glue them to the front and sides of the 'house'. Glue some greenery in place.

2. Using the diagram as a guide, measure the width of the box and twice the depth, plus two 1cm (½in) flaps at each end. Cut the grey card and lightly score the centre fold and the two end flaps.

3. Draw the roof tiles by using the black marker to rule horizontal lines about 1cm (½in) apart. Divide these with offset vertical lines. To avoid smudges, use a plastic bevel-edge ruler or set square with the flat underside uppermost. Attach double-sided sticky tape to the flaps. Remove the protective covering and attach to the top of the 'house'.

Step 2.

> **TIP:**
> You may well get carried away with this package – try adding roses round the door, a flowerbed in front and a tree on the side; we added the greenery from the packaging of a supermarket meal. Have fun thinking up new ideas.

# SUNNY MOTHER'S DAY

Traditionally, flowers are given on Mother's Day, and our hand-made sunflowers will no doubt be graciously accepted. They are easily made from double-sided crêpe paper, with a brown felt centre.

*YOU WILL NEED*

- ◆ Yellow/marigold crêpe paper
- ◆ Wire
- ◆ Small piece of brown felt
- ◆ Self-adhesive label
- ◆ Small sharp scissors
- ◆ Green crêpe paper for stems
- ◆ Compass
- ◆ Bulldog clip
- ◆ PVA glue

*METHOD*

1. Trace out the petal template. Cut a strip of yellow crêpe paper 6cm × 45cm (2½in × 17½in) and fold so the petal template will fit. Hold the template in place on the folded paper with a bulldog clip, and cut around the petals with small sharp scissors. Curl the ends of the petals over the scissors.

2. Attach the self-adhesive label to the back of the brown felt and, using the circle below as a guide, use a compass to draw a circle. Push the point of the compass through the felt to make a hole, and make another beside it. Cut out on the drawn line.

3. Run a light coating of PVA glue along the base of the strip of petals. Gather and wrap the crêpe paper petals around the wire about halfway up; squeeze tightly for a moment while the glue dries. Arrange the petals and firmly press the centre flat. Push the end of the wire through the centre hole in the felt, bend it over and return the end through the second hole. Gently slide the petals towards the felt circle.

4. Cut a narrow strip of green crêpe paper and put a dab of glue on one end. Secure the end of the strip under the flower head to cover the flower base, then wrap and stretch the paper, at the same time twirling the wire. Finish the end with a dab of glue. Make more flowers in the same way.

Wrap the gift. Cut a length of crêpe paper and 'frill' the edges by pulling them between the thumbs and fingers of both hands. Tuck the flowers under the band, holding them in place with a small piece of sticky tape.

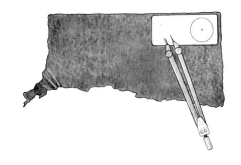

Step 1

Step 2

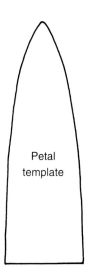

Sunflower centre template

Petal template

---

47

---

**TIP:**

As maps are made from fairly heavy-duty paper, use double-sided sticky tape to close the folds, and run finger and thumb along the folds to give a nice crisp edge.

# KING OF THE ROAD

Here is a novel idea for wrapping a guide book for someone about to take the trip of a lifetime: to cover it with a map. Out-of-date versions of 'wrapping' maps can be found in charity shops or boot sales. Or perhaps someone dear to you has been given a car as a landmark birthday present, or maybe driving lessons: a box containing the keys could be wrapped in a street map.

*YOU WILL NEED*

- An old map or a page from a street directory
- Small box for the keys
- Double-sided sticky tape
- Ribbon to co-ordinate with the roads: blue, green or yellow
- Scissors
- Small piece of white card
- Smaller piece of blue paper

*METHOD*

1. Choose an interesting area on the map, and place the edge of the book along a fold. Measure the amount needed, following the instructions on page 14, and cut to size. Remembering to place the book face down, assemble the package and finish with a co-ordinating ribbon in a simple knot, with an extra length tied over the top and all four ends curled over the blade of a pair of scissors.

2. Choose a section of the map with plenty of detail; this might relate to a familiar area, or perhaps – just to tease – to a particularly busy town.

3. The gift card is simply made from white card. Using a compass, draw two circles, just touching, and cut out. Score the fold on the right side. Draw a slightly smaller circle on blue paper. Draw an arrow on white paper and cut out. Using spray glue, attach the blue paper to the circle and add the arrow.

Step 1

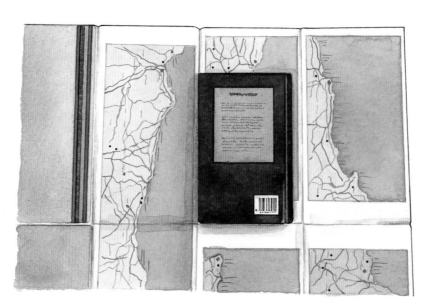

## ROMANCE RULES!

Often conceived and sent in secrecy, Valentines are always eagerly awaited on 14 February by the young and not so young alike! The traditional practice of sending hand-made cards and gifts makes this anniversary particularly appealing. The two templates have been provided with a dotted line so they can be enlarged for larger packages and other projects.

*YOU WILL NEED*

◆ Tissue paper in two contrasting colours
◆ Small sharp scissors
◆ Sticky tape
◆ Blank card 26cm × 1cm (10in×6½in)
◆ PVA glue
◆ Orange stick

**TIP:**
You may like to save the tiny cut-out hearts and use them on a card, or just add them to the envelope so that, confetti-like, they tumble out when the card is opened.

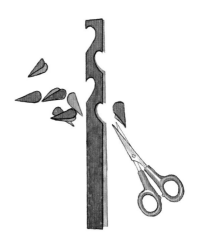

4. The Valentine card is made by attaching a 3-D heart over a piece of torn tissue. Using the larger size heart template, follow the instructions in step 2, but make wider folds in the tissue paper. Cut out at least fifteen. Spray-glue the torn tissue and place on the card. Rule a light pencil centre guideline. Attach the first heart along the pencil line, using a cocktail stick to make a fine line of dots on the centre fold. Gradually build up the layers to make a 3-D heart. The card will also need to be packaged in a box, so check that it will fit the box before you begin.

Top left: Step 2

**TIP:**
Finish with a combination bow of wide satin and narrow organza ribbons.

*METHOD*

1. Select the base colour and wrap the package in one of the tissue papers.

2. Cut the second tissue paper to fit like a band around the width of the package but to the same length as the top. Fold the tissue in half and then a couple more times until you have a narrow band of folded paper. Trace the template and cut out, then place on the folds. Draw around the half heart on opposite sides, tessellating the shapes so that they will interlock.

3. Cut out the heart shapes using small sharp scissors. Open up the paper carefully and wrap it around the package, fastening the edges at the back.

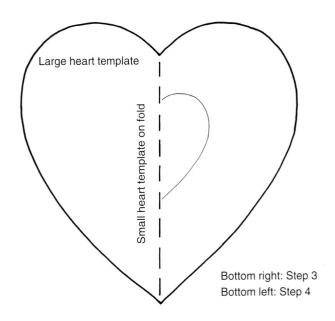

Large heart template

Small heart template on fold

Bottom right: Step 3
Bottom left: Step 4

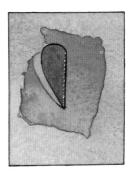

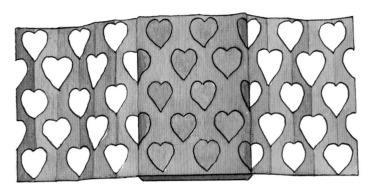

# GOLDEN DAYS

A golden wedding celebration calls for very special gift wrapping, for it is likely that all the gifts will be collected together, waiting in anticipation for the ceremonial opening. Our gift has double wrapping, a plain lining, and an outer sleeve that contains sequins and holographic sparkle trapped between two layers of transparent, self-adhesive book covering.

*YOU WILL NEED*

- Plain paper lining for the package
- Clear self-adhesive plastic
- Champagne glass and star-shaped laser sequins
- Ruler
- Tape measure
- Double-sided sticky tape
- Scissors
- Tweezers
- Gold elastic
- Very narrow and 1cm (³⁄₈in) gold ribbon

*METHOD*

1. Cover the package with the lining paper following the instructions on page 14. Using a tape, measure across the top of the box and round to the back, adding 2.5cm (1in) wrap-over. Measure the opposite direction but omit the folding area. You are making a wrap-around band.

2. Cut two pieces of self-adhesive plastic to the above measurements. Peel off the protective covering, starting from one corner. Place the sheet sticky side up on a clean surface, and hold in place at each corner with masking tape. Slide a guide under the plastic and leave a gap without sequins so that the plastic will fold neatly. Arrange the little sequins on the sticky plastic, making sure they lie flat and are well distributed. Scatter some glitter.

3. When you are satisfied with the arrangement, remove the edge of protective covering from the second piece of plastic and align the edges. Use a ruler on the top and slide it firmly along away from your body, at the same time pulling the covering off. The pressure from the ruler will release the backing paper. Smooth the film from centre to edge with the hand or a soft cloth. If there are any air bubbles, prick with a needle very close to the motif and smooth the film flat. Trim the edges to size and wrap around the package, securing the join with sticky tape.

We used gold elastic stretched round two corners and attached a length of folded gold ribbon. Build up the folds, gradually making them shorter and ending with a loop. Catch them in place with a piece of narrow ribbon and tie a knot. Attach to the package with a sticky pad.

**TIP:**
You may need a practice run at this project! Make window mount cards out of your first try.

Below: Step 2.

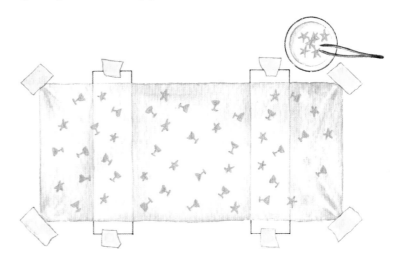

# HAPPY WEDDING DAY

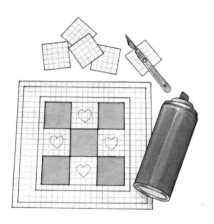

Above: Step 1
Below: Step 4

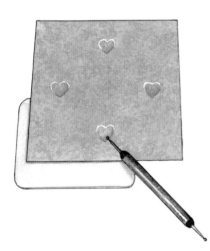

A combination of silver leaf and hand-made paper with embossed hearts, simply wrapped, with a decorative ribbon finish. The paper with its co-ordinating card will surely be saved as a beautiful reminder of the happy day. A good starter project for the delicate technique of applying silver leaf, together with an opportunity to emboss a romantic heart stencil.

## YOU WILL NEED

◆ Packet of silver leaf
◆ Pastel-coloured hand-made paper
◆ PVA glue
◆ Cream wrapping paper
◆ Graph paper
◆ Double-sided sticky tape
◆ Scissors
◆ Craft knife
◆ Ruler
◆ Soft cloth
◆ A variety of silver ribbons both wide and narrow

## METHOD

1. Cut the cream paper to fit the package and follow the basic wrapping instructions on page 14. Decide on the overall size for the decorative motif – ours was 15cm

**TIP:**
Although we used a purchased stencil, you can cut a heart shape out of card. When embossing, always work from the back with the stencil on the underside.

**TIP:**
If you know the wedding theme colours ahead of time, it would be a nice touch to wrap your presents to co-ordinate with them.

(6in). On the centre of a large piece of graph paper, make a mask by ruling a 5cm (2in) grid of nine squares (eight lines). Draw a rough guide of four hearts in alternate squares. There will be five silvered areas. Cut or tear the hand-made paper 1cm (½in) larger (16cm/6¼in square). Using a sharp craft knife and ruler, cut out the five squares intended to be silvered, and lightly spray the back to hold in place for the next step.

2. Hold the mask against the window and centre the hand-made paper, then attach to the back of the graph paper. Using a spray booth and following the manufacturer's instructions, lightly spray-glue the areas to be silvered. Leave the mask in place.

3. Keeping the protective paper on the silver, carefully cut five 5cm (2in) squares. Gently place one over the sticky square and, using a soft cloth, smooth in place. Finish the next four and carefully remove the mask.

4. Centre and hold the heart stencil in place with masking tape on the right side, making sure the tape does not touch the silver. Turn the paper over and, using a lightbox or the window, use a stylus or empty ball-point pen to trace around the edge of the four heart shapes.

The co-ordinated card was made using the above techniques, but with a wedding bells stencil.

# 4 Children

This section contains imaginative ideas for you to capture the magic of childhood. Let the children join in and learn skills that will last a lifetime.

**TIP:**
Children would enjoy the 'hills' technique but use a sponge and poster paint instead of spray paint.

# COUNTING SHEEP

An amusing way to present the gift of a sweater might be to decorate the gift wrap with a flock of sheep. Easily made and one which children would enjoy, the sheep are squares of fur fabric with their faces and legs drawn in black felt-tip pen. A torn paper mask was used to create the hills, which were spray-painted. Always use spray products in a well-ventilated room.

### YOU WILL NEED

- A box large enough for a sweater
- Pale green gift wrap
- Double-sided sticky tape
- Masking tape
- Newspaper or butcher's paper for the stencil
- Small piece of white fur fabric or felt
- Black felt-tip pen
- Green craft or car spray paint

Bottom left: Step 2.

### METHOD

1. Cut the green paper to fit the box. Lightly mark with a pencil where the top of the parcel will be, then draw guidelines marking the box off in thirds. Tear off a strip of butcher's paper wide enough to cover the green paper and two thirds of the box lid. Cover the surrounding furnishings with newspaper, or use a spray box (page 11). Use masking tape to keep the green paper flat. Either spray-glue a light coating on the reverse of the stencil, or hold in place over the green paper with masking tape.

2. Read the instructions, then shake the paint well and apply a light coat along the edge of the torn stencil. Leave to dry, then move the stencil down and across the green paper to vary the 'hills'. Spray another coat, and repeat twice more; the green will grade from dark to light. When the paint is dry, wrap the parcel following the guidelines on page 14.

3. The hills are paler in the distance. Varying the size, cut a number of small shapes from the fur fabric and apply double-sided sticky tape to the backs. Place the 'sheep' on the hills in the foreground. Use the black felt-tip pen to draw long triangles for the faces and straight lines for the legs.

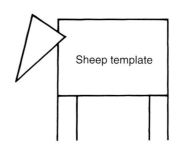

Sheep template

**TIP:**
If you do not have
a suitable cylinder,
cut a rectangle of
paper and roll it
round a bottle to
get a good curve,
then secure with
glue or sticky tape.

# WALKING THE DOG

Children and adults alike love animals, and this little dachshund is a good way of packaging a cylindrical shape. Once you have mastered the technique you will enjoy thinking up new subjects – perhaps mice or crocodiles, or you could join several together to make a snake.

*YOU WILL NEED*

- A cylinder
- Tan-coloured thick paper or thin card
- Small piece of black paper
- All-purpose gel glue
- Double-sided sticky tape
- Ruler
- Orange stick
- Scissors
- Tartan ribbon
- Two black sequins for eyes

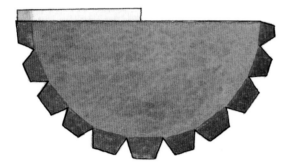

Above: Step 1.

Below : Step 2.

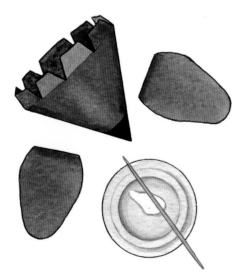

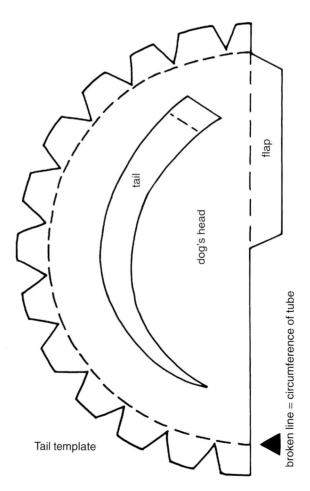

tail

dog's head

flap

broken line = circumference of tube

Tail template

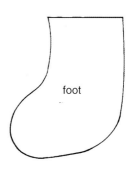

foot

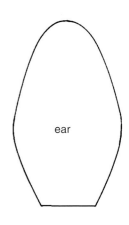

ear

If necessary, enlarge templates to fit cylinder.

*METHOD*

1. Using a tape measure, measure the length and around the cylinder (the circumference) and draw a rectangle on the tan paper with an extra 1cm (½in) overlap. Using a compass, draw a half circle the same size as the circumference of the cylinder, adding 1cm (½in) overlap on all edges. Draw a circle the same size as the opening end of the cylinder. If appropriate, enlarge the trace of the ears and feet and tail templates on this page, and transfer them onto the tan paper. Cut out all the pieces from the tan paper and trim 'v' shapes from the rounded edge of the head. Cut a small half-circle shape from black paper.

2. Roll the 'body' paper around the cylinder, and close with double-sided sticky tape. Form the head and nose shapes into cones. Close the joins on the inside with sticky tape, and stick the black nose over the end of the head. Fold the head 'v' flaps and put a small amount of glue on them before attaching on the outside of the body.

3. Roll the ears over a pencil to make them curve slightly and attach them to the head. Using an orange stick, put a thin line of glue on the overlap and attach to the outside of the cylinder.

4. Glue the legs to the body. Put the circle over the end of the cylinder and add the tail. Glue two sequins in place for eyes. Make a collar from tartan ribbon and glue over the neck joins.

# DICEY

A double six is always welcome, perhaps for a friend who enjoys board games! Easily made from black paper and sticky stationer's dots. A box that is twice as long as it is wide works best (ie 24cm × 12cm/10in × 5in).

*YOU WILL NEED:*

- ◆ Black paper
- ◆ Twelve white stationer's dots, or
- ◆ A small piece of white card and a compass
- ◆ Glue
- ◆ Double-sided sticky tape
- ◆ Small length of black-and-white ribbon

*METHOD*

1. Wrap the parcel, making the closures invisible by using double-sided sticky tape. Measure and mark with a fine pencil a guideline across the centre of the package, extending the line down the sides and onto the back. Measure and mark six equal dots on either side of the centre dividing line. If you do not have the appropriate stationer's dots, draw around a small coin or use a compass to make twelve circles. Cut out the white dots.

2. Attach the dots, using glue or double-sided sticky tape on the backs of the cut-out circles. Finish by wrapping the ribbon over the centre line to the back, closing the ends of the ribbon with a piece of sticky tape. Add a flat bow, made by folding a piece of ribbon over your hand and leaving two ends, stapling or gluing the loop in the centre. Cut

three short lengths and glue them into rings. When the glue is dry, slide them over the 'bow'. Attach with a sticky pad.

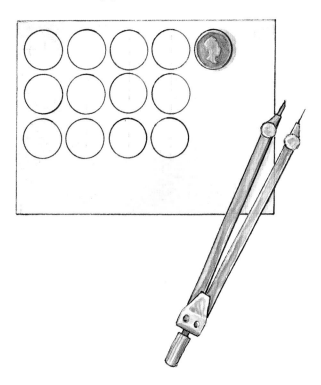

Above: Step 1.

Below : Step 2.

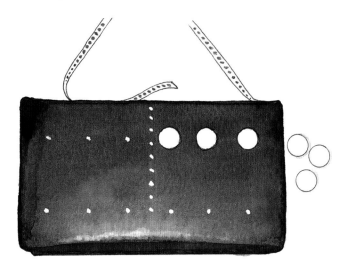

# CHEAP 'N' CHEERFUL

Sometimes we just want to be creative and present a gift using materials already in the house, to make unique wrappings with loads of effect. The following pages offer some speedy and economical ideas – in a word, recycling. It is not necessary to cover all the paper with patterns or motifs, just an area will do the trick. Some of these projects can involve the children.

*METHODS*

1. An interesting net effect can be produced by spraying car or craft paint through a piece of net supermarket orange bag, cut flat. Protect the surrounding furniture, tape the net over some coloured paper and, using short bursts, spray-paint. Leave to dry. Try manipulating the net, or using lace or paper doilies.

2. Printing with vegetables always gets results: experiment with carrots or potatoes cut into a shape, or simply cut an apple in half and print onto a base paper. We used fabric paint, but any sort of paint will work well. Tape the paper to a couple of sheets of newspaper. Use a brush to apply the paint to the apple, and press onto the paper. Use your little finger to steady your hand.

3. Not suitable for children, and do protect yourself as well as the surrounding area from splashes. Discharge patterns can be made by dropping bleach onto a dark-coloured paper. We recycled the cat's medication dropper, pouring a little diluted bleach into the bottle. Use a hairdryer to halt the discharge process. Lines, spots and drops are very effective. Have fun making patterns.

4. Dark red leaves which have been pressed in a telephone directory for a couple of weeks, can be spray-glued and then attached to the wrapping paper. Flowers can also be pressed – for a range of colours, pick and press them throughout the year.

6. Tear or cut favourite motifs from 'previously loved' paper, and stick them to a co-ordinating base paper. Use spray glue, or spread PVA on the wrong side. It is sometimes best to wrap the parcel first, just to be sure the scrap will fit.

7. Lay a piece of white paper under crumpled tissue, then paint the tissue with a bold design. The tissue will 'bleed' into the white paper, making a delicate design.

Below right:
Step 2 – Printing with fruit.

Below left:
Step 3 – Discharge method using bleach.

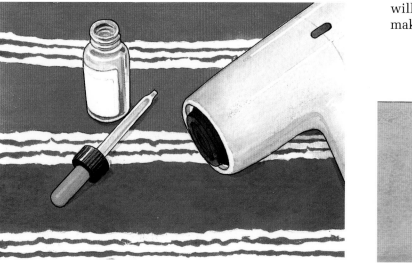

# GREEN AND BLUE PAGE

1.  You can print with leaves at any time of year. Put them in a telephone directory for a couple of hours to flatten them. Tape the paper to a pad of newspaper and then to the working surface. Select leaves in two or three sizes, lay one on a sheet of spare paper and, using a brush, apply paint to one side. Carefully turn the leaf over and place on the wrapping paper.

    Cover with a piece of kitchen roll and gently rub with your fingers. Lift the leaf up, then repeat, combining all three sizes.

2.  Interesting decorations can be made by wrapping string around a small block of wood. We made the string pattern the same measurement in both directions. Hold the wrapping paper in place with masking tape on each corner. Pour some paint into a saucer and apply to the block with a small sponge roller. Print, rotating the block each time.

3.  White layout paper provided the base for a pretty gift wrap. Protect the surrounding area and spray car paint, pressing the nozzle very gently, to produce a mixture of splashes and spray. Leave to dry, then overspray in a contrasting colour.

Step 2.

4.  You can also recycle tissue paper. Scrunch it into a ball, and then open almost flat. Spray with car or craft paint, leave to dry and then smooth out. Try folding a sheet concertina fashion, and cutting out some shapes on the folds; spray through them onto another piece of tissue: this is two for the price of one, as the cut-outs can be used, too.

5.  Photographs or postcards can have a second life if you cut them into strips and attach these to the top of a package. They also make excellent gift tags and greetings cards.

6.  The blue-on-blue stripes were achieved by the simple device of tearing random lengths of paper and using them as a stencil. Lightly coat the wrong side of the lengths with spray glue, place on the paper, then spray with car or craft paint in a lighter colour. Leave to dry. Children would enjoy sponging colour instead of spray painting with it.

7.  To transform bubblewrap, make a simple bag by folding, then sewing together the sides of a length. We used a wide zigzag stitch on the sewing machine and sprayed the bag with car paint.

Step 1 – Printing with leaves.

**TIP:**
Easiest of all: 'tease a teenager' with a 'pass the parcel' wrapped with many layers, each containing money – just about the most welcome gift you can give the young!

**TIP:**
When spray-painting, protect the surroundings with sheets of white tissue paper: the paint drift will produce extra-value spontaneous colour combinations for later use.

# 5 Christmas and Holidays

This is a time for conspicuous gift wrapping – an opportunity to be flamboyant and frivolous. Have lots of fun with glitzy materials.

**TIP:**

If the bag contents are heavy, glue a piece of reinforcing card to the outside of the base.

# IT'S IN THE BAG

It's often hard to disguise bottles and jars, so why not put them into a custom-made bag? Simple to make, just like wrapping a box but closed at one end, with the other folded to the inside, then holes punched for ribbons to be threaded through. Use any box that is roughly the right size as a 'former' for the gift. To ensure the safe arrival of the contents, choose strong wrapping paper with co-ordinating tissue for heavy items.

*YOU WILL NEED*

- Strong wrapping paper 10cm (4in) longer and 2.5cm (1in) wider than the 'former' box
- A 'former' box roughly the same size as the gift
- Double-sided sticky tape or PVA glue
- Hole punch
- A length of co-ordinating ribbon or cord
- Tape measure
- Ruler
- Craft knife

*METHOD*

1. Measure around the box and add 2.5cm (1in) to the width. Measure the length of the box and add from 10cm (4in), depending on its size (*see* 'Wrapping a Box' page 14). If the object to be wrapped is taller than the 'former', add to the length.

2. Fold in 2.5cm (1in) at the top (shorter) edge of the paper, glue in place and leave to dry.

3. Put a strip of double-sided sticky

tape on the wrong side of the length of paper. Wrap the paper around the former box, peel off the sticky tape covering and close. Fold in the bag base ends as shown in Basic Wrapping on page 14 and secure with double-sided sticky tape. Pinch along the edges to make crisp folds. Carefully slide the former box out. Centre, mark and punch holes for the handles, and thread cord or ribbon through them.

The front of the bag can be decorated by sticking on flowers or motifs.

Step 2.

**TIP:**

Any kind of box from one round a tube of toothpaste to a cereal packet can be used, but it's easier with a firm box.

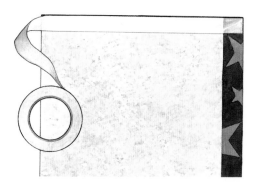

Step 3.

## PLEATED TISSUE

An elegant combination of two papers, silver and gold combine their riches. Both papers are pleated on the top of the package and also the underside, thus combining the two. Finished with gorgeous gold tassels and cord, this is a quality act. Tassels are fun and easy to make.

*YOU WILL NEED*

- Silver and gold tissue paper
- Sticky tape
- Double-sided sticky tape
- A box for the gift
- Two skeins of gold metallic-stranded embroidery thread
- One skein of silver metallic-stranded embroidery thread
- Scissors
- A piece of card measuring 9cm (3½in) in one direction
- Masking tape
- Comb

*METHOD*

1.  Measure the papers to fit the package as described on page 14, but add at least another 12cm (5in) to the length of the silver and 6cm (2½in) to the gold. Make two concertina 3cm (1¼in) folds on one end of the right side of both the papers.

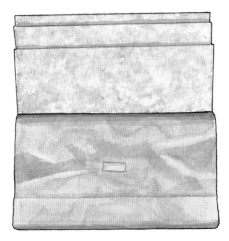

Step 1.

2.  Wrap the longer (silver) paper around the box, finishing with the pleats in the centre on the right side. Hold in place with sticky tape. Arrange the pleats of the silver paper beside the gold pleats and wrap the paper round to the back, folding in the edge so that both gold and silver can be seen. Attach double-sided tape to close. Put some small pieces of double-sided sticky tape under the folds. Finish and secure the ends in the usual way.

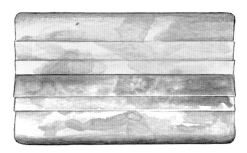

Step 2.

3.  Tassels: wrap the whole skein of embroidery thread around the card. The thread will be rather springy, so hold it in place with a small piece of masking tape. Cut one end and carefully lay the strands out flat.

Step 3.

4.  Find the middle of the strands and bind the silver thread smoothly around them until the centre is covered. Gently bend the centre and bring the strands together, binding around the neck of the tassel. Secure the end by sewing in, but hold temporarily with a piece of masking tape while you thread the needle. Remove the masking tape. Comb the threads until they are smooth, then cut the ends neatly. Attach to a hand-made (page 28) or purchased silver and gold cord.

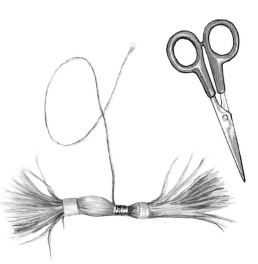

Step 4.

**TIP:**
As every box will be a different size, work out the amounts you need with some old paper first. You may need to vary the size of the pleats, depending on the size of the package.

# SNOW TRACKS

Paper folding need not be origami. Try folding tissue or good quality paper into triangles, then more triangles, then open the paper and discover an intricate network of pattern. Flatten the paper slightly and use stencil paint to print along the folds. We used silver on a dark blue paper.

*YOU WILL NEED*

- Either dark or light tissue or good quality wrapping paper
- Dry stencil paint in silver or a darker colour
- Stencil brush
- Sheet of butcher's paper to cover the table
- Scissors
- Masking tape
- Bevelled-edge ruler
- Silver ribbon

*METHOD*

1. Cut the wrapping paper into a large square and fold diagonally from corner to corner. Run the clean bevel edge of a ruler along the crease. Fold again and repeat until the paper is quite small.

2. Open out the paper and smooth it, but do not flatten it out. Hold the paper still with a small piece of masking tape at each corner. Following the instructions for dry stencil paint, brush, with a stabbing movement, along the creases, taking care not to overfill the brush. Start with the area furthest away from you. It's best to make the first brush stroke onto a spare piece of paper to remove the excess paint; mop it up later when the brush begins to empty. Apply a second coat and press harder to make darker marks. When the painting is complete, leave the paper to dry.

Take care not to pick up paint on your fingers: keep a cloth handy to wipe them at frequent intervals.

Wrap the present in the usual way – if there are any extra pieces of the patterned paper left, use them on a gift card. We tore an area from an offcut and applied it with spray glue onto a metallic card.

**TIP:**
This technique could be used on cotton fabric: fold and press with a steam iron to get good crisp folds.

**TIP:**
Remember all those complicated paper-folding games from your childhood? Well, use them again for patterning paper.

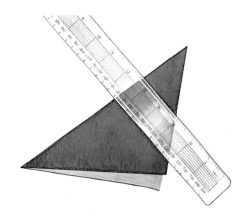

Step 1.

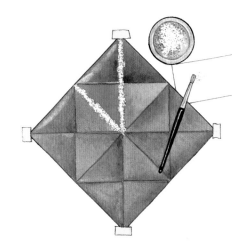

Step 2.

# YOU'RE AN ANGEL

A very unusual way to deliver a double gift. The small present is hidden inside the angel's skirt – just untie the bows, pull the silver thread – and out it will tumble! Sew either by hand or machine. The angel is then ready to sit atop the festive tree.

## YOU WILL NEED

- An old-fashioned wooden clothes peg
- White paint
- A small piece of dupion silk 16cm × 28cm (6½in × 11in)
- A small square of fine cotton 6sq cm (1½sq in)
- Needle and white thread
- Tiny piece of cotton wool
- 10cm (4in) silver ribbon
- Yellow embroidery thread
- Red and blue coloured pencils, sharpened to a fine point
- Silver card 8cm × 10cm (3in × 4in)
- Silver thread

## METHOD

1. Paint or spray the wooden clothes peg white. Using the diagram of the angel's dress as a guide, make a pattern, and cut out from the silk. Cut out the head circle from the white cotton. Using double thread, sew a gathering stitch around the circle and draw up slightly. Sew a narrow hem at each end of the angel's dress, then pin, right sides together, and sew across the ends of the 'sleeves' and down the sides with a small running stitch. Turn through to the right side.

2. Cut a small hole in the centre of the dress to make a neckline. Gently push the head of the clothes peg through. Wrap some cotton wool over the peg and cover with the white circle, pulling the threads tight around the 'neck'. Manipulate the gathers towards the back of the head. Bind with thread to cover the rough edges, and carefully tuck them into the neckline.

3. Draw in the features using the coloured pencils. Cut some strands of yellow embroidery thread to approximately 6cm (2½in). Using an orange stick, dot a line of PVA glue along the angel's 'centre parting' and stick the hair in place. Gather one edge of the ribbon to make a neck frill and tie it in place. Fold the angel's arms in front and secure with a stitch. Fashion a small gift from beads or ribbons for her to hold.

4. Trace the wings' template (page 90) and transfer (page 43) to the silver card, cut out and attach. Tuck the present inside the skirt and, using silver thread, sew the two sides together with large stitches. Leave long tails at either end and tie in bows.

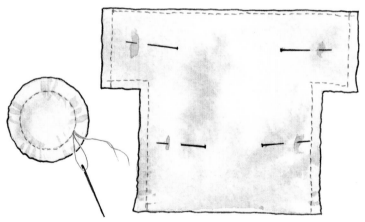

Step 1.

# RING OUT THE BELLS

Bells are meant to be heard, in the past to warn of danger, but now more usually to call the faithful to church, as well as to celebrate weddings, Christmas and New Year. We have chosen traditional Christmas colours for our bells, the small versions worked in a circle, the larger as decoration or gift tags. The two parcels are colour co-ordinated and could form a theme for hand-made Christmas cards as well.

*YOU WILL NEED*

- Green tissue and red hand-made paper
- Corrugated gold card
- Red card
- Strip of gold paper 24.5cm × 4cm (9¾in × 1½in)
- Co-ordinating ribbons
- Double-sided sticky tape
- Small sharp scissors
- Red sequins
- Co-ordinating red and gold ribbons in a variety of widths, including wire-edged
- Hole punch

*METHOD*

1.  Wrap the parcels (page 14). Trace the larger bell template and transfer to a piece of card. On the reverse of the gold and red cards, draw around the edge and cut out. Punch holes in the top of the bells. Cut a length of the gold net ribbon long enough to knot and leave tails. Wrap it in one direction and tie. Add the red and gold striped ribbon in the opposite direction, finishing with a large bow. Punch a hole and thread the curled ribbon through the gold gift tag.

2.  Wrap the package in green tissue paper in the usual manner. Fold the strip of gold paper in half, then in half twice more. Trace out the smaller bell shape and draw around it onto the gold paper. Cut out using small scissors, making sure not to cut off the bottom corners of the bell. Carefully unfold the strip, spray-glue the backs, and attach the bells in a circle to the package. Stick a sequin onto each bell, then wrap a narrow ribbon diagonally round two corners. Add a larger bell gift tag with a co-ordinating ribbon.

TIP:
Use tissue paper double thickness to make the colours more intense.

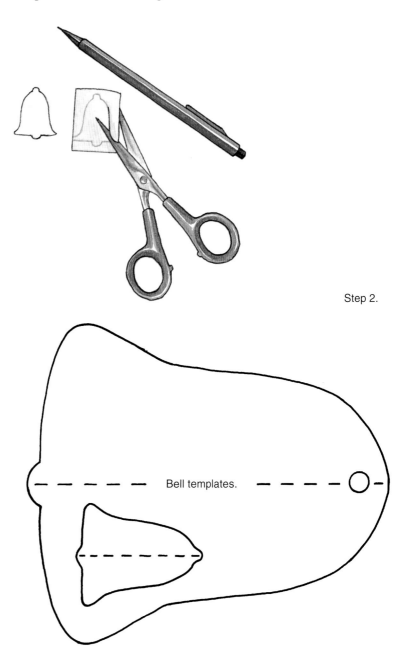

Step 2.

Bell templates.

# PYRAMIDS OF TREASURE

Transfer chocolates and sweeties from their packaging, and make them look a million dollars by presenting them in acetate or pearlized card pyramids. Our template helps to make quick work of the project.

*YOU WILL NEED*

- ◆ Pearlized card or acetate (A3 size will make several)
- ◆ Double-sided sticky tape
- ◆ Sharp craft knife
- ◆ Ruler
- ◆ Sharp pencil
- ◆ Tracing paper

*METHOD*

1.  To make a small box 10cm (4in) high, trace the template on page 89. To make larger sizes, photocopy the template. The broken lines are scoring and folding guides, the continuous lines are for cutting.

2.  Draw around the template and transfer the design onto the card. On the right side, score the eight fold lines using the back of a craft knife. Cut out. On the right side attach a narrow strip of double-sided sticky tape to the flap.

3.  Decorate, if you wish, with felt-tip pens, sequins, dots and squiggles and so on. When the ink or glue is dry, peel off the tape cover and, starting from the point, carefully stick the pyramid shape together.

4.  Fill with sweets and chocolates and fold the base flaps to close. Hold in place with a decorative sticker. Add curled ribbon decorations.

A greetings card using the same template will complete the gift. We hand-coloured stationer's dots with felt-tip pen.

> **TIP:**
> Enlarge the template on page 89 to 170 per cent to make a pyramid 17cm (6¾in) high; or enlarge to 130 per cent for one13cm (5in) high.

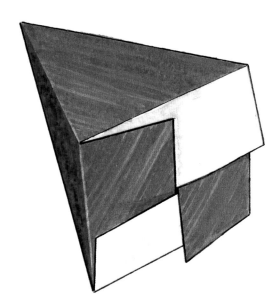

Step 2.

## STRIPES, DOTS, STARS AND SQUIGGLES

Christmas is a wonderful opportunity to use glitzy materials and to go over the top with gift wrapping. Here we have combined several ways of creating effects from the theme of red and gold. Painted stripes, dots and stars drawn with gold pen and contour paint gold squiggles are just some suggestions. Once you start painting, more ideas will occur – the theme could be continued for a festive occasion with greetings cards and table decorations. Don't worry if the odd smudge appears: this merely serves to verify that your wrapping paper is made by hand, not by machine. Finally, go to town with ribbons.

*YOU WILL NEED*

♦ Dark red wrapping paper
♦ Gold gouache paint
♦ Sharp pencil
♦ Ruler
♦ Water jar
♦ Palette
♦ Flat paintbrush
♦ Masking tape
♦ Thick gold felt-tip pen
♦ Gold contour paint
♦ A variety of gold and red ribbons, including wire-edged, in several widths

*METHOD*

1.  Measure the package and cut the paper to fit. Place the paper on a flat surface and, to prevent it moving, hold it in place with a piece of masking tape on each corner. Using a fine-tip pencil, rule guidelines about 4cm (1½in) apart. Mix some paint on the palette with a tiny drop of water. Load the paintbrush and in one long sweep, paint the first line. Start from the left side if you are right-handed so that you do not smudge the painted lines, from the right if you are left-handed.

2.  Dots and stars: hold the paper in place with masking tape on each corner. The spots and stars are drawn freehand, using a thick gold marker. Shake the pen well and press down on the tip a couple of times to release the gold ink.

3.  Contour paints are marketed for use on fabric, but they will also work on paper. Hold the paper in place with masking tape. Using the template as a guide, draw wavy lines and fill in the curves with a spot. The paint will take some time to dry (a couple of hours), after which the colour will become brighter. If you feel impatient, use a hairdryer.

Finish the packages by decorating with a variety of red and gold ribbons, trinkets and baubles.

**TIP:**
When using contour paints on wrapping paper, work out where the folds and overlap edges will occur and keep the design on either side.

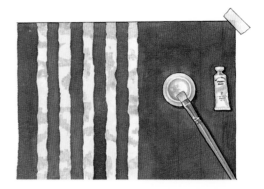

# CRACKING GOOD FUN

Traditionally crackers are filled with small gifts, a joke or pun and a paper hat. As they are pulled, eyes are screwed shut in preparation for the snap! Our reusable cracker is intended as a centrepiece to decorate a festive table, and it is large enough to accommodate gifts for everyone, as well as paper hats and mottos. Add a snap if you wish. It will become a family favourite for years to come.

*YOU WILL NEED*

- A 'former' tube about 8cm (3¼in) in diameter and cut to about 61cm (24in) long ensures a smooth cylinder shape
- Lightweight card, 29cm (11½in) wide, two × 8cm (3in), three × 20cm (8in)
- Two snaps joined together with sticky tape
- PVA glue
- Two sheets of white crêpe paper cut 29cm × 42cm (11½in × 16½in)
- Green crêpe paper cut 20cm × 30cm (8in × 13in) and two pieces 6cm × 30cm (2¼in × 12in)
- Silver paper
- 1m (3ft) × 8cm (3in) wide nylon lace with a gathering thread on one side
- 56cm (22in) narrow silver ribbon
- 30cm (12in) silver ribbon 4cm

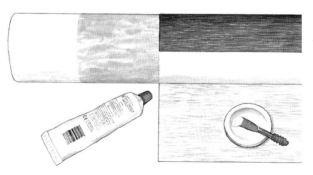

Step 2.

(1½in) wide
- 36cm (14in) wired cord
- Craft knife
- Stapler
- Fine string
- A4 sheet of tinsel paper
- Needle and thread
- Gifts and mottos

*METHOD*

1. Roll one of the larger pieces of card around one end of the former, glue and hold in place with elastic bands. Roll a centre section around the former, mark with a pencil where the overlap falls. Slide the former out slightly and, using the stapler upside down, insert a staple. This will ensure the smooth side of the staple is inside the cracker. Take the roll off the former and insert more staples; use sticky tape if the stapler is too short. Make the other three

**TIP:**
As you will require two formers, one slightly fatter than the other, it will be simpler to make one end of a tube larger by wrapping and securing some thin card around it.

**TIP:**
Avoid wrapping the cracker card too tightly around the former, as space is needed for the crêpe paper turn-in.

**TIP:**
For a good source of puns, buy a book of schoolboy jokes. Snaps can be purchased from craft shops.

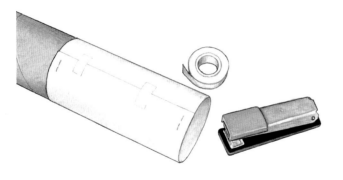

Far left: Step 1.
Left: Step 3.

Step 4.

Step 5.

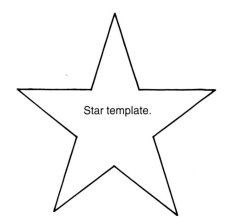

Star template.

tubes the same way, but use the fatter end of the tube for the remaining larger piece.

2. Lay one sheet of white crêpe paper on a flat surface, and arrange one set of completed cylinders (on the former) with a 10cm (4in) gap between, and a 2cm (¾in) turn-in at each end. Check the join will fall on top of the staples. Using a spatula, apply PVA glue sparingly along one edge, taking care not to get it on the former. Applying slight tension, close the edges. Repeat for the other end, keeping the middle section on the fatter section of the former. Remove when the glue is dry; apply PVA to the ends and fold in.

3. Wrap the green crêpe paper around the larger centre section and secure. Using the template as a guide, cut the crown shapes and apply to the ends of the cracker. Add nine circles, cut from silver paper or card, to the points on each crown point. We used a hole punch. Glue the silver ribbon to the ends.

4. Slide one end of the cracker onto the former and support the overhanging section. Wrap a length of fine string around the space between the middle and end of the cracker, and pull tightly but gently, gathering up the crêpe paper. Tie a knot and trim the string. Pull the gathering thread in the lace into a circle, place around the cracker and knot the ends. Repeat for the remaining piece.

5. For the final decorative touch, draw and cut out seven circles 8cm (3in) in diameter. Fold the circles in quarters and cut bold 'v' shapes from around the edge. Sew through the folded centre and arrange the segments in a ball. Sew the pom pom firmly onto the centre of the silver ribbon and wrap it around the cracker, securing the ends with glue.

Cut three lengths of wire cord. Cut out six stars, using the template as a guide. Put one end of the wired cord between two stars and glue them together. Curl the wire around a pencil. Make two more stars in the same way and glue the ends inside the silver pom pom.

**TIP:**
Card will roll more smoothly in one direction, so experiment on a spare piece before starting on the project.

# GIFT TAGS

Making a little gift tag does not take long, but fun can be had making one to continue the gift-wrapping theme, echo the contents, reinforce the colours, or use as an opportunity for a special message. Here we show a selection of ideas to make your present memorable. Templates for tags marked with an asterisk can be found overleaf. Many other gift-tag ideas accompany the gift-wrap projects.

Holly leaf made from metallic card, which has been scored on the wrong side. Stationery dot berries have been added.*

A golden tassel with the details scored using a dry ballpoint.*

Balloons always signal festivities: to add sparkle, tie a thread around the 'opening'.*

Snowflakes are made from a piece of thin paper cut into a 9cm (3½in) square. Fold twice more into a tiny square. Cut off the corners and cut 'v' shapes into the sides. Open up and divide the square into four snowflakes. Spray-glue the back and attach to a darker colour card.

Make the Christmas tree by folding a small square of mulberry paper in half and cutting a triangle and beneath it a small square. Spray-glue to a small contrasting colour card.

Deckle scissors give a dainty edge to gold card mounted on pale lavender.

Simple-to-cut stars are cut from pearlized card.

The heart shape is cut from hand-made paper using deckle scissors.

Your message can be written around the spiral, cut from lavender card.*

Mount the two halves of the Easter egg on a piece of card and cut around the edge.

Use an unthreaded needle in the sewing machine, or a darning needle to punch holes in the hexagon.*

# Templates

Spiral.

Hexagon.

Tassel.

Four circles.

Holly.

Balloon.

Easter egg.

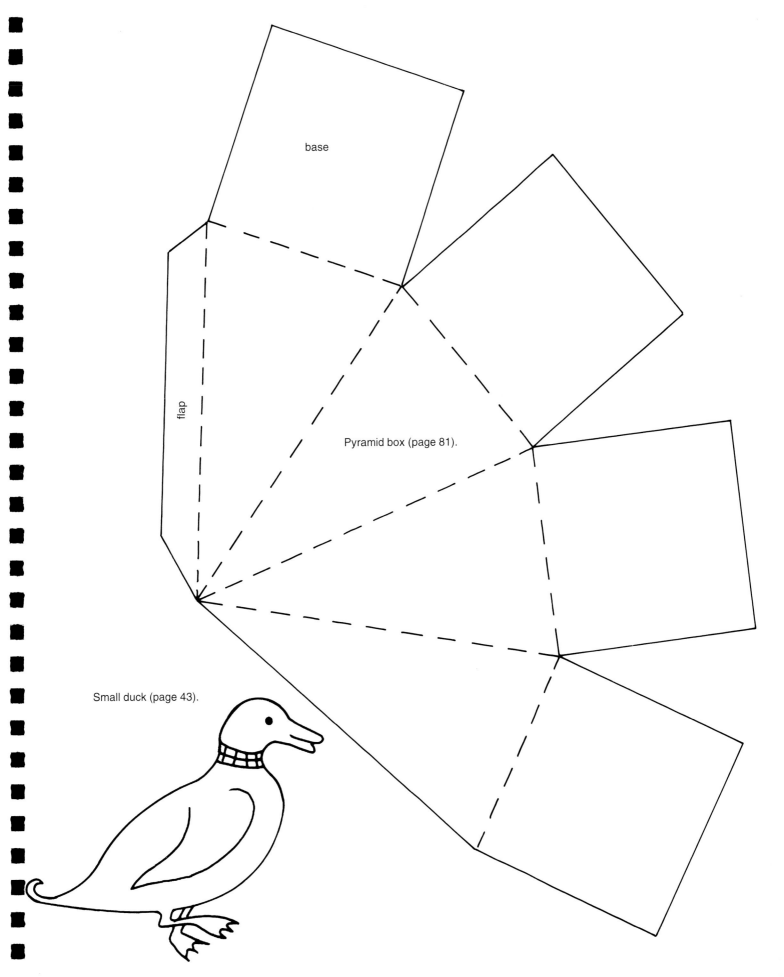

base

flap

Pyramid box (page 81).

Small duck (page 43).

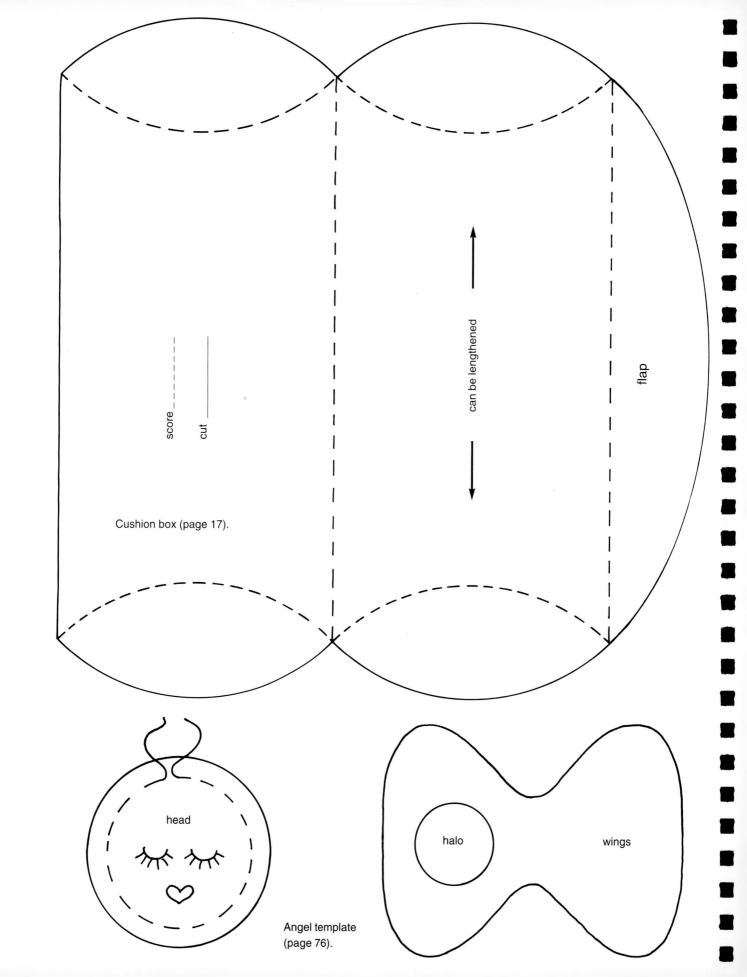

score

cut

can be lengthened

flap

Cushion box (page 17).

head

halo

wings

Angel template
(page 76).

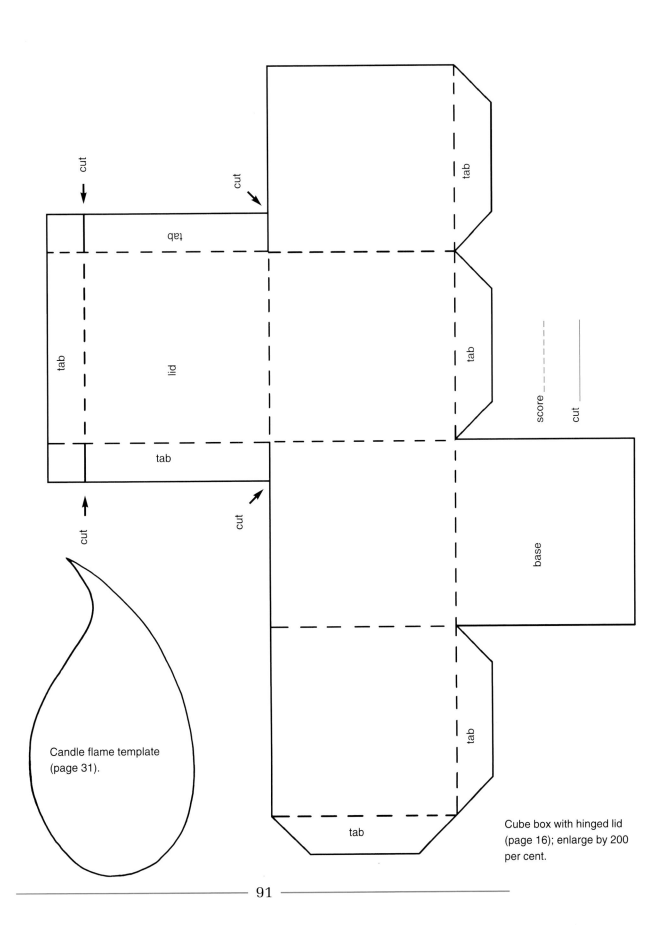

cut

cut

tab

tab

tab

tab

lid

tab

tab

score ------

cut ———

base

cut

cut

tab

Candle flame template (page 31).

tab

Cube box with hinged lid (page 16); enlarge by 200 per cent.

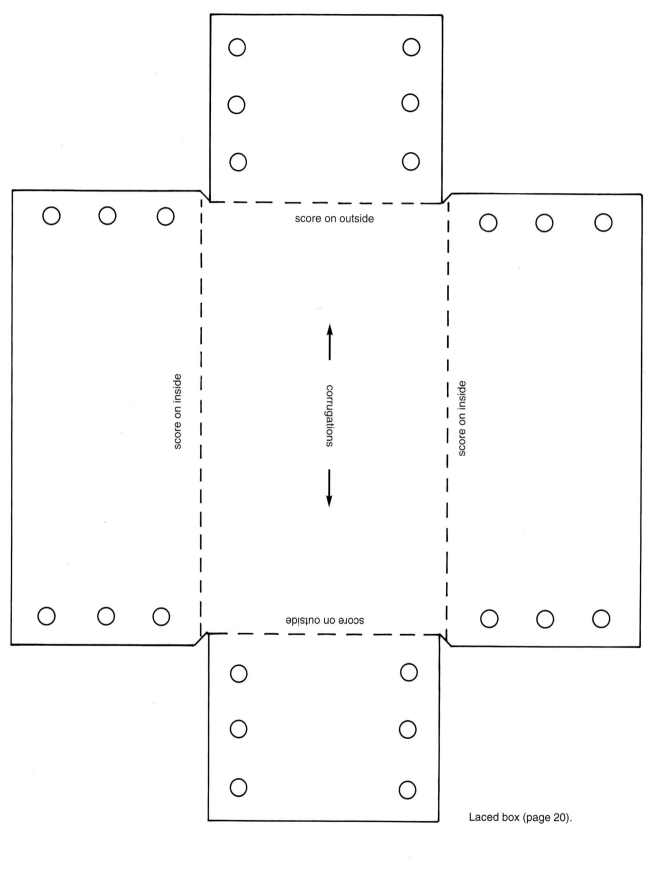

score on outside

score on inside

corrugations

score on inside

score on outside

Laced box (page 20).

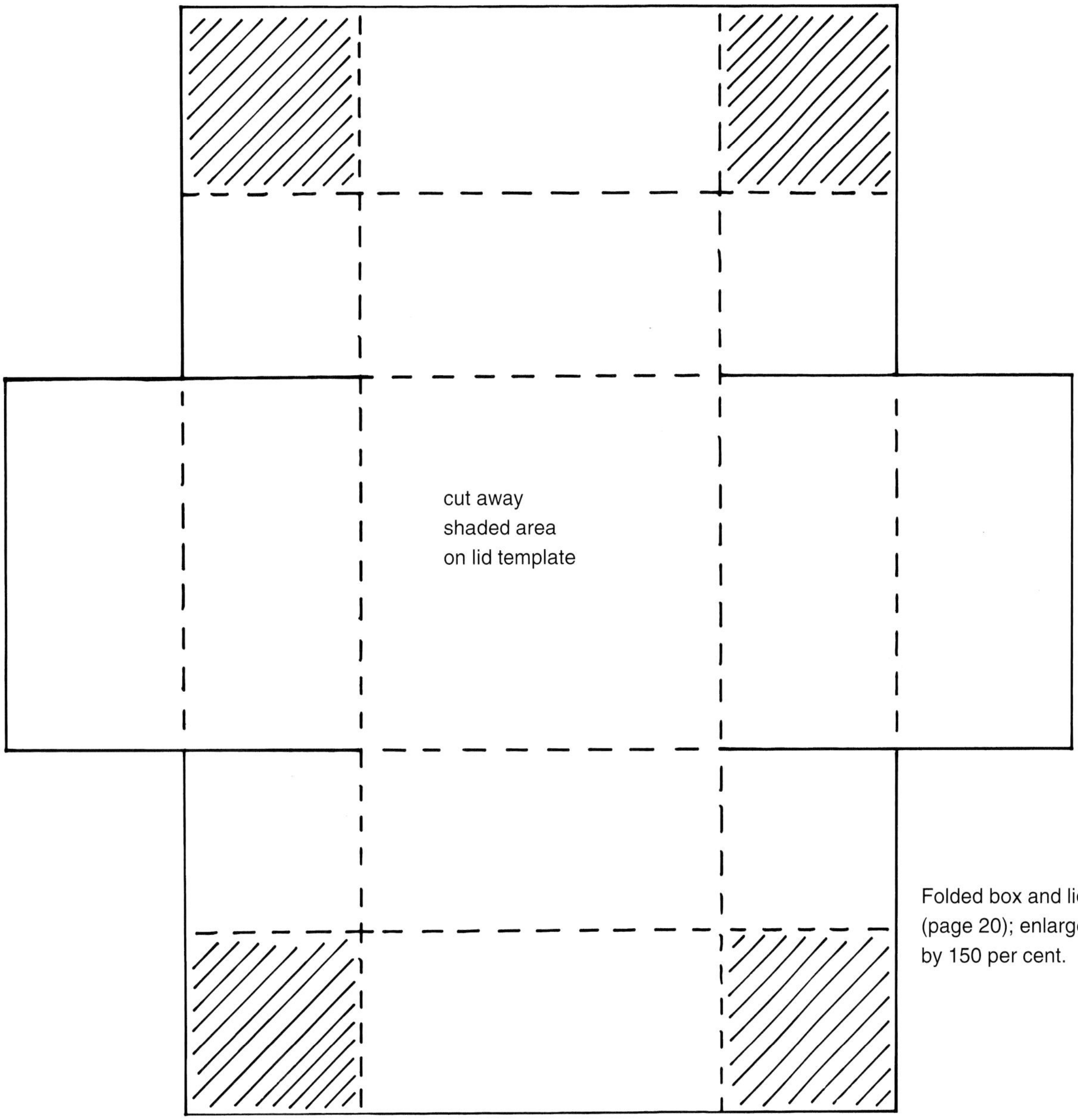

cut away
shaded area
on lid template

Folded box and lid
(page 20); enlarge
by 150 per cent.

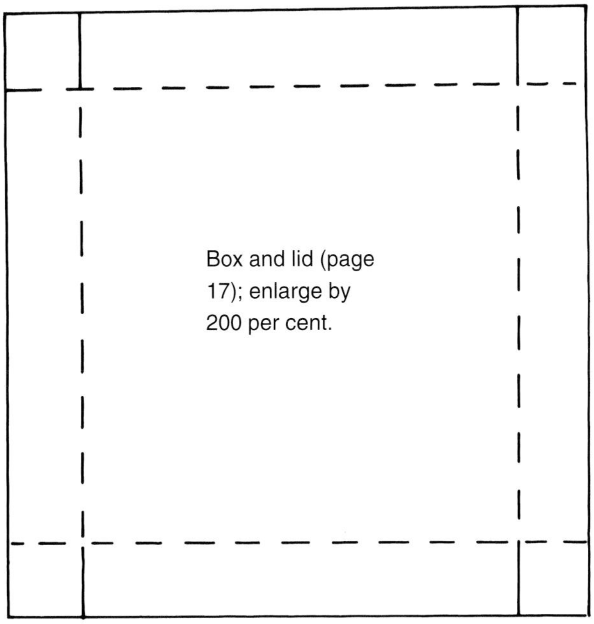

Box and lid (page
17); enlarge by
200 per cent.

# Stockists

## UNITED KINGDOM

Art Van Go
16 Hollybush Lane
Datchworth
Knebworth
Herts SG3 6RE
Tel: 01438 814946
*Mail Order: Silver leaf, hand-made paper, paints and dyes*

Coats Crafts UK
PO Box 22 Lingfield
McMullen Road
Darlington
Co. Durham DL1 1YQ
Tel: 01325 381010
*Coton à Broder thread*

Craft Creations Ltd
Ingersoll House
Delamare Road
Cheshunt
Hertfordshire EN8 9ND
Tel: 01992 781900
*Card and Paper*

Crafty Ribbons
3 Beechwood
Clump Farm
Tin Pot Lane
Blandford
Dorset DT11 7TS
Tel: 01258 455889
Fax: 01258 456060
*Mail order: Wide range of ribbons*

Creative Grids
PO Box 207
Leicester
Leicestershire LE3 6YP
Tel: 0116 285 7151
*Mail order: Cutting mats, template plastic*

DMC Creative World Ltd
Pullman Road
Wigston
Leicestershire LE18 2DY
Tel: 0116 281 1040
*Stranded embroidery thread*

Dylon International Ltd
Worsley Bridge Road
London SE26 5HD
Tel: 020 8663 4296
*Dyes and paints*

Imagina Clarity Stamps
Ludwells Farm
Spode Lane
Cowden
Kent TN8 7HN
Tel: 01342 850111
*Mail order: Stamps and ink pads*

Paperchase Products Ltd
213 Tottenham Court Road
London W1P 9AF
Tel: 020 7580 8496
*Paper, card and art materials*

The Pier
3 Elmfield Road
Broadway Corner
Bromley
Kent BR1 1LW
Tel: 020 8466 8099
*Household and gifts*

P & Q Stencils
Oak Tree Cottage
Evesbatch
Bishops Frome
Worcestershire WR6 5BE
Tel/Fax: 01531 640001
email: dihuck@aol.com
*Mail order: Stencils, dry stencil paints, brushes, embossing tools*

Fashion 'n' Foil Magic
PO Box 3746
London N2 9DE
Tel: 020 8844 1992
Fax: 020 8883 0845
email: info@fashionfoil.com
www.fashionfoil.com
*Mail order: Foil papers, templates, rubber stamping, sequins*

UHU(UK) Ltd
551 London Road
Isleworth
Middlesex TW7 4DS
Tel: 020 8847 2227
*Adhesives*

## USA

C & T Publishing Inc/Fox Hill Workshops
1651 Challenge Drive
Concord, CA 94520-5206
*Gift Wrap Books*

Loose Ends
PO Box 20310
Salem
OR 97307-0310
*Papers and ribbons, also fragment package containing pieces of papers and ribbons*

Sax Arts & Crafts
PO Box 510710
New Berlin
WI 53151
*Paints, papermaking and embossing materials*

New York Central Art Supply Co.
62 Third Avenue
New York,
New York 10013
*Hand-made paper, papyrus, artist's supplies*

Decorative Papers
PO Box 749
Easthampton
MA 01027

## SOUTH AFRICA

Art & Graphics Supplies
169 Oxford Road
(Nedbank Centre entrance)
7B Mutual Square
Rosebank
Johannesburg

X-Press Graph-X
29 Siemert Road
Doornfontein

Crafty Supplies
32 Main Road
Claremont
Cape

## AUSTRALIA

Janet's Art Books Pty Ltd
143 Victoria Avenue
Chatswood
NSW 2067

Handworks Supplies
121 Commercial Road
South Yarra
VIC 3141

## NEW ZEALAND

Gordon Harris
4 Gillies Avenue
Newmarket
Auckland

Littlejohns
170 Victoria Street
Wellington

# Index